FREDERICK THE GREAT, BISMARCK,

and the Building of the German Empire in World History

Tom McGowen

Enslow Publishers, Inc.

40 Industrial Road	PO Box 38
Box 398	Aldershot
Berkeley Heights, NJ 07922	Hants GU12 6BP
USA	UK

http://www.enslow.com

Library of Congress Cataloging-in-Publication Data

McGowen, Tom.
    Frederick the Great, Bismarck, and the building of the German Empire in world history / Tom McGowen.
        p. cm.—(In world history)
    Includes bibliographical references and index.
    ISBN 0-7660-1822-9
    1. Frederick II, King of Prussia, 1712-1786. 2. Prussia (Germany)—Kings and rulers—Biography. 3. Prussia (Germany)—History, Military 4. Prussia (Germany)—Politics and government—1740-1786. 5. Bismarck, Otto, Fèurst von, 1815-1898. 6. Statesmen—Germany—Biography. 7. Germany—Politics and government—1848-1871. 8. History, Modern—18th century. 9. History, Modern—19th century. I. Title. II. Series.

DD404 .M34 2002
943'.042'092—dc21

                                                    2001004210

Printed in the United States of America

10 9 8 7 6 5 4 3 2 1

To Our Readers: We have done our best to make sure all Internet addresses in this book were active and appropriate when we went to press. However, the author and the publisher have no control over and assume no liability for the material available on those Internet sites or on other Web sites they may link to. Any comments or suggestions can be sent by e-mail to comments@enslow.com or to the address on the back cover.

Illustration Credits:
© Corel Corporation, p. 59; Enslow Publishers, Inc., pp. 4, 58, 64, 108; Hulton Archive/Getty Images, p. 74; John Grafton, *The American Revolution: A Picture Sourcebook* (New York: Dover Publications, Inc., 1975), pp. 56; National Archives and Records Administration, pp. 86, 115; Reproduced from the Collections of the Library of Congress, pp. 16, 21, 39, 42, 50, 55, 62, 76, 83, 89, 98, 101, 104.

Cover Illustration: Enslow Publishers, Inc. (Background Map); Hulton Archive/Getty Images (Frederick the Great portrait); Reproduced from the Collections of the Library of Congress (Bismarck portrait).

Contents

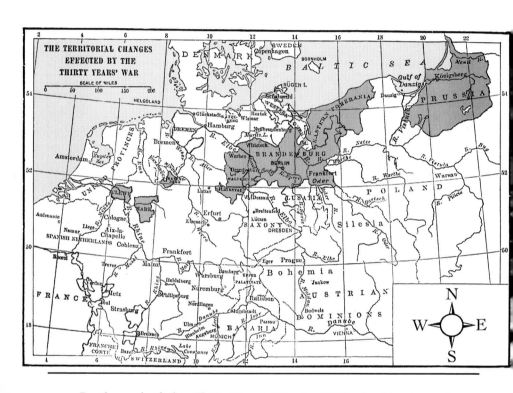

By the end of the Thirty Years' War in 1648, the kingdom of Brandenburg-Prussia (shaded) had emerged in Europe.

Chapter 1

The Crown Prince of Prussia

Some twenty-five-hundred years ago, the region now called Germany was the home of a number of barbaric warlike tribes. One of these tribes called itself the Germani, but the people of the ancient Roman Empire called all the tribes Germani, and named the region Germania. The name stuck.

By the beginning of the 1700s, the lands of the tribes had become many little countries, independent cities, and tiny bits of land ruled by kings, princes, dukes, and even bishops. The people of these little states all spoke the German language, with different dialects from place to place, but they thought of themselves as Württembergers, or Hessians, or Saxons, rather than Germans. They all were part of what was called the Holy Roman Empire, which consisted of what is now Germany, Austria, Slovakia, the Czech

Republic, and parts of Poland and Belgium. When an emperor of this empire died, the new emperor was actually elected by the rulers of many of the little German countries, who were known as electors. At the beginning of the 1700s, the emperor was Charles VI of Austria, a German-speaking country that had many of the customs of its Germanic neighbors.

One of the small German kingdoms was known as Brandenburg-Prussia. It was an odd country, because some parts of it were not even connected to the rest. It was in the northern part of what is now Germany, and was formed mainly of three provinces, or states—Brandenburg, Pomerania, and East Prussia. East Prussia was separated from the other two provinces by a small part of Poland called West Prussia, and two other tiny bits of the kingdom, Cleves and Minden, also lay some distance away, to the west. The Kingdom of Brandenburg-Prussia was not regarded as being of much significance by most people of Europe.

However, Brandenburg-Prussia was destined to be the heart of the unified nation of Germany that exists today. This was due to the efforts of two Prussian leaders, King Frederick the Great and Prime Minister Otto von Bismarck, who did their work nearly a hundred years apart from each other. Frederick the Great helped Prussia become the major kingdom of Germany. Bismarck then helped Germany to become a single unified nation.

The capital of Brandenburg-Prussia was the city of Berlin, in Brandenburg, and it was there that the royal palace stood. In Berlin's royal palace, a prince was born into the Prussian royal family, the Hohenzollerns, on January 28, 1712. He was named Karl Frederick, but everyone soon began calling him just Frederick, which was also the name of his father and grandfather, the king.

A year after Frederick's birth, his grandfather died and his father became King Frederick William I. This meant that little Frederick was now the Prussian crown prince, who would become the next king after his father. He had a sister, Wilhelmina, who was two years older, but being a female, by law she could never become Prussia's ruler. Eventually, Frederick had ten brothers and sisters altogether, but as the oldest boy, he was always the one to inherit the throne.

The Creation of a Military Machine

Frederick William I was a stout, quick-tempered man who firmly believed that God had given him the right to be a ruler and that he could do whatever he wanted. However, he was not a tyrant or an oppressor, and he tried to do his best to improve his kingdom and the lives of his people. However, his main interest was the army of forty thousand men his father had left him. "I find pleasure in nothing in this world save in a strong army,"[1] he once declared. He was determined that through discipline, little Prussia would have an army capable of defending the country against anyone. So, he began to virtually turn his soldiers into machines. They were trained to instantly obey orders, to march all in step at a steady pace, to quickly and smoothly change direction at a command, and to be able to stand and shoot like machines, no matter how much danger they were in.

The weapon of the soldiers who fought on foot, the infantry, was the smoothbore musket (three feet, eleven inches), which was fired from the shoulder. It shot a lead ball (one ounce), and had to be reloaded after each shot.

Loading was a rather complicated process. The lead ball came wrapped in a paper container called a cartridge, which also contained a quantity of gunpowder. To load the gun, a soldier took a cartridge out of a leather pouch slung from his shoulder and hanging at his right hip, and tore it open with his teeth. He sprinkled a bit of powder from the cartridge into a small opening, called a pan, on the musket barrel (the metal tube the bullet comes out of) above the trigger. He covered the pan. Then he slid a long rod, called a ramrod, out of its socket under the barrel, and used it to quickly push the powder-filled cartridge and ball all the way down to the bottom of the barrel. The ramrod was then slid back in its socket. The firing mechanism, called a flintlock and consisting of a hammer-like device holding a piece of flint stone, was cocked by pulling it back. A spring held it in place. The soldier lifted the musket to his shoulder and pulled the trigger. The spring was released, causing the flintlock to snap forward. The flint hit the steel edge of the pan where powder had been sprinkled into, making sparks that ignited the powder. The flash of the powder, which exploded with a loud snap, ignited the powder-filled paper cartridge that exploded with a louder BANG, sending the lead ball whizzing out of the musket.

In addition to the slowness of reloading, soldiers of most armies were also hampered by having to use ramrods made of wood. A wooden ramrod soon got bent, and had to be handled carefully so it would not break, which would leave the musket useless. This made reloading even slower. But Frederick William I equipped his soldiers with iron ramrods, and then trained them to load their muskets rapidly and efficiently. Thus, while the infantry of most armies could fire only two shots a minute, the Prussian infantry became able to fire five times a minute. This would be a big advantage in a battle.

So as young Prince Frederick grew up, he was used to the snap-BANG of muskets going off and the machinelike tramp of marching feet as Prussian soldiers drilled and trained on the parade grounds outside the palace.

An Abused Prince

For the first seven years of his life, Frederick was cared for mainly by two women, a governess (a woman entrusted with the care of a child) and a tutor (a private teacher). One of these ladies was French. From her, he learned how to speak and read French, and gained a liking for French ways that stayed with him all his life. By the age of seven, Prince Frederick was a thin, smallish boy who stood and walked slightly stooped over. Now, his father ordered that his care be taken over by men, officers of the Prussian Army who would teach him military ways. One of his toys was a miniature arsenal (military storehouse), with tiny cannons, ammunition wagons, and other objects of military life.

As a teenager, Frederick was still smallish and stooped, not a bit like his large, chubby father. And he was taking a direction that his father did not care for. Frederick steeped himself in the art, music, and literature of France, and seemed to regard German ways as barbaric. He learned to play the flute and became a skilled musician. He wrote several pieces of music that are still played to this day by symphony orchestras. But he did not seem in the least interested in the Prussian Army or in military ways, as his father was.

It was soon clear that his father did not like him very much. Frederick William I treated the young prince violently, shouting at him, shoving him, and often striking him with his cane. At dinner time, if the crown prince did or said something that angered the king, the king was likely to throw a plate or bowl at the prince's head. On one occasion, the king became so enraged by something Frederick had done that he actually choked the boy with a tasselled curtain cord.[2] Frederick began to despair. "I am treated like a slave,"[3] he declared to Wilhelmina, who was also sometimes treated harshly by their father.

When he was eighteen, Frederick tried to run away. He and a nineteen-year-old man named Hans von Katte, who was his best friend, made plans to slip away to the border on horseback and leave Prussian territory. Frederick intended to go stay in England, where his uncle was King George II. But the plan was discovered, and the crown prince and his friend were arrested by order of Frederick's father. The enraged king had Frederick's friend beheaded and put Frederick in a cell to also await execution. Throughout Europe, people wondered if the wild king of Prussia would actually have his crown prince executed.

Eventually, the king calmed down and Frederick was released. For a time he was put to work doing boring office tasks and was not allowed to read any French books, play his flute, or eat anything but very plain food. But gradually, the king relented. After about a year, he appointed Frederick to colonel in the Prussian Army and gave him his own infantry regiment, titled the Crown Prince Regiment. Frederick began to spend time training and drilling his regiment and began reading books on military history. This was part of the upbringing of young European noblemen, for they were expected to become the commanders of their countries' armies.

In 1733, the king arranged for Frederick to be married to the daughter of the count of Brunswick, Elizabeth Christina. This was not Frederick's choice, but for a while he seemed happy with his new wife.

Source Document

I have not ventured for a long time to present myself before my dear papa, partly because I was advised against it, but chiefly because I anticipated an even worse reception than usual and feared to vex my dear papa still further by the favor I am now to ask; so I have preferred to put it in writing.

I beg my dear papa that he will be kindly disposed toward me. I do assure him that after long examination of my conscience I do not find the slightest thing with which to reproach myself; but if, against my wish and will, I have vexed my dear papa, I hereby beg most humbly for forgiveness, and hope that my dear papa will give over the fearful hate which has appeared so plainly in his whole behavior and to which I cannot accustom myself. I have always thought hitherto that I had a kind father, but now I see the contrary. However, I will take courage and hope that my dear papa will think this all over and take me again into his favor. Meantime I assure him that I will never, my life long, willingly fail him, and in spite of his disfavor I am still, with most dutiful and childlike respect, my dear papa's.

Most obedient and faithful servant and son
Frederick[4]

The relationship between Frederick and his father was often a tense one, as this letter from Frederick to the king shows.

However, after a time he began to live by himself and seldom visited her.

From Crown Prince to King

A year after Frederick's marriage, the Holy Roman Empire became involved in war with France. Prussia supplied the Imperial Army with a force of ten thousand men, and Frederick William I sent Frederick along with them. The king seemed to want to find out if Frederick was at all capable of being a soldier.

It quickly became obvious that Frederick was not the least bit frightened or concerned about being in a battle. When he and several other officers were sent out to spy on enemy troop positions, French artillery began shooting at them. Frederick carried on a conversation with one of the other officers, not paying the least attention to the cannonballs smashing into trees all around him. He was also learning how to command troops in a battle, and how to pick the best places to fight a battle so that he would have an advantage. Hearing of all this, Frederick's father was very pleased. Gradually, he became more and more friendly toward his eldest son. In 1735, he made Frederick a major general.

On the last day of May, in 1740, King Frederick William I died. At the age of twenty-eight, Crown Prince Frederick was now King Frederick II of a small, unimportant kingdom that was tenth in size among the kingdoms of Europe. But the well-trained, well-equipped army of eighty-three thousand men his father had created for the kingdom, was actually the fourth largest army in Europe.

Most people of Europe expected that Frederick would simply reduce the size of the army in order to save money and would devote himself mainly to music and culture. For a time, it looked as if they were right. Frederick appointed some new officials, passed some laws—one of which abolished torturing criminals to gain confessions—and did some traveling. He became friends with one of the greatest writers and thinkers of those days, the Frenchman Voltaire. Voltaire said

Source Document

Well, now, is it better for your fatherland to be a monarchy or a republic? For four thousand years has this question been debated. Ask the rich for an answer, they all prefer aristocracy; question the people, they want democracy; only kings prefer royalty. How then is it that nearly the whole world is governed by monarchs? . . . the real reason is . . . that men are very rarely worthy of governing themselves. It is sad that often in order to be a good patriot one is the enemy of the rest of mankind. . . .[5]

Voltaire, one of the most famous philosophers of the era called the Enlightenment, was friendly with Frederick II.

of Frederick, "I became fond of him; he had wit and charm."[6]

But people began to notice that Frederick was actually building up and reequipping the Prussian troops. They were being brought together and organized as if for war. Everyone wondered what Frederick was up to.

On December 16, six and a half months after becoming king, Frederick showed them. Leading an army of twenty-seven thousand men, he invaded Austrian territory and started a war.

Frederick the Great

A Surprise Victory

The Austrian emperor, Charles VI, had died in October. He had no sons, only two daughters. By law, neither of them could become ruler of the empire. However, the emperor had tried to make arrangements with most of the electors to accept his eldest daughter, twenty-three-year-old Maria Theresa, and her husband, the duke of Lorraine, as emperor and empress. Some leaders of the empire were willing to agree to this, but others were not. The ruler of one of the German nations, Charles Albert of Bavaria, believed he had a better right to rule the empire than Maria Theresa did, and was threatening to go to war about it. The powerful kingdom of France seemed willing to help him. Thus, Austria was facing the possibility of a serious war.

Frederick had decided to take advantage of this situation. With the Austrian Army having to prepare for a war in the west, it might not have enough troops to spare for a problem to the north. Brandenburg had an old claim to the northern Austrian province of Silesia (now part of Poland), so Frederick led his army into Silesia and began taking it over to make it part of his kingdom. He put troops in many Silesian towns, where they could control the countryside. In effect, he seized Silesia from Austria. This was the beginning of what was to become known as the First Silesian War.

Source Document

A well conducted government must have an underlying concept so well integrated that it could be likened to a system of philosophy. All actions taken must be well reasoned, and all financial, political and military matters must flow towards one goal: which is the strengthening of the state and the furthering of its power. However, such a system can flow but from a single brain, and this must be that of the sovereign.[1]

Frederick the Great explained his theory of how a government should be run.

18

By the end of January, 1741, the Prussian army had occupied most of Silesia. But despite her problems with Bavaria and France, Maria Theresa certainly did not intend to just give up Silesia to Frederick. In March, an Austrian army of about sixteen thousand men marched into the province with the purpose of pushing the Prussians out. Frederick gathered his army together to meet the Austrians. On April 10, on a snow-covered field near a little town called Mollwitz, the two armies faced each other.

The Way of War in 1740

To a person of the twenty-first century, an eighteenth-century battle would seem somewhat like a parade with explosions. Even the uniforms were more like parade uniforms than battle clothing. They were brightly colored and decorated with strips of lace and gold braid. The Prussians wore uniforms consisting of black three-cornered hats trimmed with white edges; long-tailed blue coats with cuffs and lapels of red, yellow, white, and other colors; and tight-fitting white or yellow knee-length breeches and long stockings, covered by black or white thigh-length buttoned leggings. The Austrian uniform was similar, but their coat color was white.

During the battle, there was no quick movement, no running, no attempt to take cover in any way. Infantry moved and fought in formations called battalions, composed of from six hundred to one thousand men, generally arranged in three rows, called ranks. Each rank was about one hundred twenty five yards long, with about three feet between them. If a battalion was being attacked, the men of the front rank knelt down on one knee, the second rank stooped into a crouch, the third rank stood upright, and they all pointed their muskets at the oncoming enemy. If a battalion was making an attack, it marched forward in perfect alignment, each man carrying his musket straight up, resting against his shoulder. The Prussians marched in unison at a steady pace, taking exactly the same number of steps, seventy-five, every minute. Each battalion was accompanied by a small band of drummers and fifers playing marching music to help the men keep in step. It was exactly like a parade until the shooting started.

Armies at this time were mainly formed of three "arms"—infantry, cavalry, and artillery. The main arm was the infantry, with its musket and bayonet—the long, sharp-pointed blade attached to the end of a musket, making it a deadly spear. In most armies, infantry battalions were trained to fire their muskets all together, at the command of an officer. This was called a volley, and it was much like a burst of fire from a present-day machine gun—it sent hundreds of bullets ripping into a formation of enemy soldiers at the same instant. A volley was generally fired at an enemy no more than thirty to forty yards away, and it could result in a large number of dead and wounded men. However, between each volley there was a short period of about forty seconds, while the men reloaded

Empress Maria Theresa of Austria ruled during the time of Frederick the Great.

their muskets. This, of course, enabled the advancing enemy troops to get a lot closer before they were fired on again.

The Prussians were trained to do things differently, however. An infantry battalion was formed of ten groups of seventy men each, called platoons, and instead of a single volley all at once, Prussian battalions fired platoon volleys, one after another. This meant that troops facing a Prussian battalion were constantly under fire, for by the time the last platoon fired, the first had reloaded and was ready to fire again.

Like the infantry, the cavalry—soldiers on horses —was organized in units of six hundred to nine hundred men, called regiments, formed in a number of ranks. The weapon of the cavalry was a sword, used for hacking or stabbing. To make an attack—a charge—a cavalry regiment moved forward with the horses walking for several hundred yards, went into a trot for several hundred more yards, and at a distance of about eighty yards from the target, broke into a gallop, with the riders leaning forward, arms extended and swords pointed straight ahead. Often, the very sight of those lines of horses rushing toward them was enough to make an infantry battalion dissolve in panic, with the men running in all directions.

The artillery weapon was the cannon. A cannon was a very large gun mounted on a wooden cart with wheels, which could shoot a large projectile for eight hundred to nine hundred yards. The main kind of projectile used was a solid iron ball, weighing three to twelve pounds, depending on the size of the gun. Such a projectile, rushing through the air at great speed, could wipe out four or five men at a time in a row of soldiers, smashing their bodies and tearing off arms and legs. Another type of projectile was a hollow, gunpowder-filled iron ball with a burning fuse, which would explode and send fragments of iron whirring through the air in all directions. Cannons could also fire a projectile known as grape shot, which sent a cluster of dozens of small lead balls whizzing at a line of enemy soldiers. A cannon was loaded and fired much like a musket, with a load of powder rammed down the barrel and a ball rammed down on top of that. Then, the glowing tip of a burning piece of rope was touched to a hole in the top of the barrel to ignite the powder. It could fire only one shot at a time, and only about two times a minute.

Because of the kind of gunpowder used at that time, cannon fire or a volley of musket fire threw up an enormous amount of smoke that generally hung close to the ground, like a fog. Known as "the fog of war," it rapidly spread over a battlefield, making it hard to see more than a few yards ahead. Thus, a standing battalion might suddenly see an enemy force looming out of the smoke only yards away.

A Bad Beginning

The Prussian and Austrian armies at Mollwitz were about the same size in number of men, but the

Austrians had twice as much cavalry. Frederick set up his army with the infantry battalions in two long lines, one behind the other, about three hundred yards apart. He put most of his cavalry to the right of the infantry, the rest on the left. His sixty cannons were lined up in front of the infantry. The Austrians set their force up so that their infantry was facing the Prussian infantry, and their cavalry faced the Prussian cavalry.

The Prussian cannons opened up, firing on the Austrian cavalry. The air became thick with smoke. To add to the fog of war, a strong wind was blowing clouds of snow off the ground. Suddenly, out of this wall of heavy gray mist exploded the front ranks of Austrian cavalry regiments, charging into the Prussian cavalry.

The Austrian cavalry was made up of very good, experienced troops. They had fought in a number of battles in Italy and other places. The Prussian cavalry-men had never been in battle before. Caught by surprise, they were simply swept away and scattered in all directions.

Things looked very bad. Only the Prussian infantry and a small bit of cavalry were left to face the whole Austrian Army. Prussian General Kurt von Schwerin rode up to Frederick and informed him that he had better leave the battlefield and seek safety. Grim-faced, Frederick galloped away, leaving von Schwerin in command.

The Austrian cavalry regrouped itself into its formations and prepared to destroy the Prussian infantry regiments that still stood unmoving on the snow-covered field. To the sound of bugles, the Austrians moved forward to charge and shatter the Prussian infantrymen.

But the cavalrymen ran into something they had never encountered before. The Prussian infantrymen had not ever been in battle, but they had been trained to not move without an order. They were more afraid of disobeying than of getting killed. So, as the Austrian cavalry trotted toward them, the Prussian infantry simply stayed in place and waited. When they received the order to start shooting, they began the steady fire they had been drilled and drilled to give.

Crash! From each battalion, seventy bullets from the first platoon slammed into the cavalrymen, slicing into horses and men. An instant later: Crash! Another seventy bullets from the second platoon ripped into the advancing horsemen. And an instant after that: Crash! Another seventy bullets struck. The front rows of Austrian cavalrymen turned into piles of screaming, kicking horses and dead and wounded men. The horsemen behind them could not advance through this turmoil and were forced to come to a halt. They turned their horses around and rode several hundred yards to the rear, to form up their ranks and try again.

The Triumph of the Prussian Infantry

During the rest of the morning and into late afternoon, the Austrian troops tried four more times.

The outcome was always the same. They were brought to a standstill as the well-trained Prussians poured hundreds of bullets into them, five times a minute. Finally, with their general and most of their officers now dead, the remaining Austrian cavalrymen simply refused to make any more charges. They pulled back, out of the battle.

Now, nothing was left in front of the Prussians but Austrian infantry battalions. Obeying the shouted orders of their commanders, the Prussian battalions began to march forward. Men went down here and there, hit by Austrian bullets, but the other soldiers ignored them, stepping over them, and continued forward. Thus, the Prussian battalions flowed forward with a steady crash, crash, crash of muskets rolling along the line.

Like the cavalry, the Austrian infantry could not stand against this steady blast of bullets smashing into them every few seconds. They were able to fire no more than one or two volleys, and by then the Prussians were on them, with their muskets thrust straight out so that the bayonets projected forward, a long line of sharp, glittering points. The Austrian battalions began to dissolve, as many men turned and ran. By now the sun was setting, and the Austrian commanders hurried to get their troops off the field, away from the steadily advancing Prussians and their withering blasts of fire. Hours later, messengers found Frederick and informed him that the Prussian infantry had turned what seemed an Austrian victory into an

Austrian defeat. It had been a very close battle—the Austrians had lost forty-four hundred men and the Prussians forty-six hundred—but Prussia had won the Battle of Mollwitz. Of General von Schwerin, Frederick later said, "Without him, I should have been done for; he alone repaired the mistakes and won the battle."[2]

Chapter 3

Another War, More Victories

Frederick learned some valuable lessons from the Battle of Mollwitz. Never assume that a battle is lost until it actually ends. Never leave a battlefield while there is still a chance of doing something that might turn a defeat into a victory. He also realized that the Prussian cavalry was not very dependable, and set about reorganizing and training it.

When news of the Prussian victory at Mollwitz spread through Europe, there was astonishment. It was much as if, today, a little country such as Venezuela were to fight a battle against the United States and win.

However, an Austrian army was still in Silesia, and it received reinforcements. But then Bavaria and France declared war and invaded upper Austria with the purpose of defeating Maria Theresa and making

Charles Albert of Bavaria emperor. They were taking advantage of the diversion Frederick had provided to go after their own aims. The Austrian army in Silesia had to go help fight these invaders.

This left Frederick free to do pretty much as he wanted. By spring of 1742, he had moved his army out of Silesia, into the adjoining Austrian province of Moravia. But then, an Austrian Army moved against him, and he withdrew back into Silesia.

The Austrians followed and attacked Frederick's force near the town of Chotusitz. Both sides had about thirty thousand men. Frederick arranged his army with most of his cavalry on the right, a small force of about seventy-two hundred infantry on the left, just outside Chotusitz, and a large force of about fourteen thousand infantry in the middle. But the middle force, which Frederick himself was commanding, was hidden in a low-lying area where it could not be seen by the Austrians.

The Austrians advanced against Frederick's cavalry with their own cavalry, backed by infantry. Frederick ordered his cavalry to charge. Twenty squadrons of Prussian cuirassiers—men wearing chest armor and helmets—smashed into the front line of Austrian cavalry and swept it away. But then the Prussians had to halt in order to get back into formation, and while they were halted, they were charged by several regiments of Austrian cavalry. It was their turn to be swept away. There was no longer any Prussian cavalry on Frederick's right.

On the left, Austrian infantry and cavalry advanced toward the Prussians outside Chotusitz, with a large number of cannons keeping up a steady, pounding fire on the Prussians. The Prussians fell back into the town, but the Austrians began setting fire to houses. To escape being trapped in a blazing village, the Prussian soldiers had to pull back once more, behind the town. Things seemed to be going badly for the Prussian army.

Frederick Wins His First Victory on His Own

But now, Frederick brought his force out of hiding. To the astonished Austrians, scores of Prussian battalions suddenly appeared out of nowhere, marching methodically forward, with that terrible, endless crash, crash, crash, of musket fire pouring into everything in front of it. Within minutes, just as at Mollwitz, the Austrian Army was falling back, withdrawing from the battlefield. It was another Prussian victory, and this time it was due entirely to Frederick's leadership. The Austrians had lost 6,330 men; the Prussians had lost 4,800.

Maria Theresa gave up and signed a peace treaty with Frederick, giving him full rights to Silesia. As a result of Frederick's first war, a richly fertile region of 1.3 million people had become part of Brandenburg-Prussia. Frederick had doubled the size of his kingdom.

The war between Austria and France and Bavaria continued, and by the summer of 1744, Austria was clearly winning. Suspecting that if Austria did win,

Maria Theresa would quickly try to take Silesia back, Frederick decided to provide some help to the Bavarians and French. In September, with seventy-one thousand men, he invaded the Austrian province of Bohemia (now Slovakia and the Czech Republic), hoping to force Austria to send part of its army there. This was the beginning of what is called the Second Silesian War.

To get into Bohemia, Frederick had to march his army through one of his neighbors, the little German kingdom of Saxony (now part of northern Germany). The Saxons were not able to prevent this, but they bitterly resented it. They regarded Prussia as an enemy from then on.

Bohemia was undefended, and the Prussians quickly captured the large, important city of Prague. Then they began to march southward, toward Austria, capturing towns and fortresses and leaving small units of troops in them to keep them under control. However, in October Frederick learned that an Austrian army had entered Bohemia and a Saxon army was marching to join it, for Saxony had now become Austria's ally against Prussia. This meant the Prussian army in Bohemia would be badly outnumbered. With harsh winter weather settling over the land, Frederick began pulling his troops out of Bohemia into his province of Silesia. But Austrian cavalry was now on their heels, and Frederick lost a lot of men to their quick hit-and-run attacks.

So, as 1745 began, Frederick had to start building up his army in Silesia. He did this as his grandfather and father had built up their armies, mainly by hiring foreigners who were willing to become soldiers for pay. Most of these men were wandering vagrants without jobs, and many were actual criminals, but if they could march and fire a musket, Frederick could use them. Once they were in the Prussian Army, they were subjected to the hard drill and harsh discipline that turned them into the kind of soldier Frederick wanted. Thus, while about half of the men in the Prussian Army were Prussians—generally poor peasants who could not make a living any other way—the other half were usually foreigners.

By April, Austria had made peace with Bavaria, and France had pulled out of the Austrian war in order to use all its resources to fight its old, most hated enemy, England. Prussia was suddenly facing the entire might of Austria, plus its Saxon allies, all by itself.

The Great Victory of Hohenfriedberg

On May 26, an army of forty thousand Austrians and nineteen thousand Saxons invaded Silesia. Frederick pretended to retreat northward, back to Prussia. But when the enemy encamped near the Silesian town of Hohenfriedberg, Frederick marched there during the night of June 3 with sixty thousand men. He personally scouted the enemy position, then formed his army for battle, hidden behind a little stream. At sunrise on the morning of June 4, he attacked and caught his opponents by surprise. They were spread out and unready for a battle. The Austrian commander was sound asleep in bed.

On the right, the Prussian cavalry crossed the stream and soon was involved in a swirling hand-to-hand battle with Austrian cavalry and some Saxon infantry battalions. Further downstream, twenty-one Prussian infantry battalions also crossed the stream and moved toward a line of Saxon infantry that was trying to get into formation. Steadily advancing despite vicious fire from the Saxon cannons, the Prussians got into musket range and began their steady, murderous fire. The Saxons found themselves being slaughtered, and began to melt away.

When Frederick learned that the Saxons were falling back he shouted, "The battle is won!"[1] He was right. By eight o'clock A.M., the Austrians were pulling back everywhere, and by nine o'clock it was all over. The Prussians had 4,571 men killed and wounded, but the Austrians had lost three times that many—13,800 killed, wounded, or captured. The remains of the Austrian-Saxon Army fled out of Silesia back into Bohemia. Hohenfriedberg was a tremendous victory for Prussia.

Much of Frederick's success came because he personally went out and carefully examined the countryside and scouted the positions of his enemies. He generally did this all by himself, which was a source of worry to his generals. They feared he might be captured or even killed by enemy troops who caught him alone. Once, he nearly was captured, but he hid under a bridge while enemy cavalry clattered across overhead. Frederick was prepared to take his own life rather than be captured. At all times, he carried with him an oval metal box containing eighteen poisonous pills with which he could commit suicide if he felt it necessary.[2]

The armies of the European nations at this time were all commanded by noblemen—kings, princes, dukes, or counts. These were wealthy and privileged men, who liked to show off their position by wearing expensive clothing glittering with gold braid. But Frederick always wore a common blue Prussian Army coat that was actually slightly shabby and discolored with brown stains from snuff (powdered tobacco). Despite this, Frederick's soldiers always recognized him. When he would ride through an encampment, men would call out, "Good morning, Fritz," the German nickname for anyone named Frederick. The king was not at all bothered by such familiarity. He would call back, "Good morning, children," generally with a smile. Frederick appreciated that these men were willing to die for him and Prussia, and they appreciated that he was always in the middle of battle, sharing the same danger they did.[3]

A Hard Victory at Soor

After Hohenfriedberg, Frederick had to split his army. He kept twenty-two thousand men to follow the defeated Austrians into Bohemia in hope of catching up to them and wiping them out. He sent the rest to deal with another Austrian force that was coming into Silesia from the south. But by September, the Austrian army in Bohemia had been reinforced to about forty-one thousand, and on September 30, it attacked Frederick's much smaller army near the Bohemian town of Soor. The Austrians managed to get around the rear of Frederick's force, cutting off its line of retreat.

The Prussians were in serious danger of being surrounded. The Austrians and Saxons were strung out in a long line on high ground with a forest behind them. At the left end of the line was a steep hill on which there were more than ten infantry battalions and sixteen cannons. Around the hill was a mass of cavalry. But it was here that Frederick made his attack. Five regiments of Prussian heavy cavalry charged toward the hill, caught the Austrian cavalry standing still, and pushed it back into the woods. Behind the cavalry came Prussian infantry battalions. As they moved up the hillside, balls from the sixteen cannons smashed bloody gaps in the front ranks, driving the leading battalions back. But eventually, eleven battalions reached the top, pushed the Austrians off, and captured the guns.

At that moment, the rest of the Prussian infantry, stretched out in a line facing the enemy infantry, moved forward. A bayonet charge by a Prussian Guard battalion—special troops sworn to guard the king, with a reputation for bravery and fighting skill—broke open the center of the Austrian line. When Frederick hurled a cavalry charge against the right end, the remaining Austrian cavalry and infantry fled back into the forest. The Battle of Soor was over. Both the Prussian and Austrian armies had about four thousand casualties, but the Prussians took some three thousand Austrian prisoners. It was another Prussian victory, but another very close one. Writing about it to a friend, Frederick said, "I have never been in such a fix as at Soor."[4]

Winter Battles and a Growing Reputation

With winter coming on, Frederick withdrew his army back into Silesia and put his troops into winter quarters. This meant finding places in villages for troops to stay during the winter, repairing and storing equipment, and gathering supplies. He expected the Austrians to do the same, but the Austrians and Saxons had hatched a daring plan to invade Prussia during the winter and capture Berlin. An Austrian army marched into Saxony to join Saxon forces waiting there and begin an advance into Prussia.

Frederick learned of this and quickly moved into Saxony with an army. On November 23, near a town called Hennersdorf, a portion of Frederick's cavalry moving ahead of the army ran into six thousand Saxon cavalry moving in advance of the Austrian force. The Prussians attacked and scattered the Saxons, taking nine hundred prisoners. The Austrian commander decided not to continue on, and instead headed west toward a town called Kesselsdorf, where an army of twenty-five thousand Saxons and six thousand Austrians was waiting. A portion of Frederick's force, thirty-one thousand men under General Prince Leopold of Anhalt-Dessau, was near Kesselsdorf, and Frederick sent word to Dessau to hit the Saxons and Austrians before the main Austrian force could join them.

On December 15, Dessau attacked. The Prussian battalions had to charge up a hill and were pushed back with frightful losses. The Saxons and Austrians believed the Prussians were beaten, and surged down the hill to finish them off. But Prussian cavalry that had been kept out of sight came smashing into the Saxons and Austrians from the side, cutting them to pieces and scattering them. Dessau had won the battle. When the commander of the main Austrian force heard of this new Prussian victory, he turned his army around and retreated into Bohemia.

In fourteen months of battles, Austria had not been able to gain a thing against Frederick. Maria Theresa asked for peace, which Frederick granted. Silesia was still part of Prussia, and Frederick had shown he was one of the best generals in Europe. It was now that his people began calling him Frederick the Great.

Chapter 4

Prussia Against Europe

The sudden rise of Prussia as a major military power was a cause of great concern to many European nations. Austrian diplomats were able to convince leaders of some of these nations that Prussia had to be destroyed for the safety of Europe. By 1756, Austria, Saxony, Russia, France, and Sweden had formed an alliance to fight Prussia. Great Britain, a major power among European nations, was Prussia's only ally. Great Britain was allied with Prussia simply because both nations were fighting France. Great Britain was fighting for control of North America and India; Prussia was fighting because France was allied with its main enemy, Austria.

Rather than let his enemies all come at him at once, Frederick struck first. He had expanded his army to one hundred fifty thousand men, and in

This cartoon pokes fun at the major leaders in Europe, depicting them as boxing one another for control of territory. At center are a very slim Frederick the Great and a much heavier Catherine the Great, empress of Russia.

August 1756, he marched into Saxony with seventy thousand. By doing this, he had started yet another war. This one would become known as the Seven Years' War.

America was involved in this war, on the same side as Frederick. At this time, the American colonies were still part of the Kingdom of Great Britain, which was allied with Prussia. In America, British and American troops were fighting troops of France, Britain's oldest enemy and now Frederick's enemy as well. The French were being assisted by a number of American-Indian tribes, and thus, this is known in the United States as the French and Indian War.

In Saxony, Frederick's army pushed the little fourteen-thousand-man Saxon Army into a corner, surrounding it with twenty thousand men. Then he moved to intercept a fifty-thousand-man Austrian army that had come to help the Saxons, forcing it to retreat. Saxony surrendered, and Frederick took the entire Saxon Army into his Prussian Army, replacing the Saxon officers with Prussians.

In April 1757, Frederick invaded Bohemia with sixty-five thousand men and headed for Prague, where about seventy thousand Austrian troops were encamped. On May 6, he attacked. The Austrians formed a line for battle, and Frederick hit the left side of the line with infantry and the right side with cavalry. Austrian troops began moving to each side to meet the attacks, and this opened up a gap in the middle of the line. Frederick pushed the main part of his army into the gap and split the Austrian force in two. The shattered Austrians fled into the city, which Frederick surrounded with his army. This was a procedure known as a siege, in which an army kept a city surrounded until it ran out of food and had to surrender.

Dark Days for Prussia

An Austrian army of sixty thousand men was sent to force the Prussians to end the siege. On June 18, Frederick attacked it with thirty-two thousand men, but was defeated, with more than thirteen thousand casualties to the Austrians' nine thousand. He was forced to give up the siege and withdraw from Bohemia.

Now, the whole alliance against Prussia began to move. A force of 30,200 French troops and almost 11,000 German troops from regions opposed to Frederick began marching through Saxony toward Prussia. A hundred-thousand-man Russian army invaded the Prussian province of East Prussia. A small Swedish army invaded the Prussian province of Pomerania. An Austrian army of one hundred ten thousand was advancing into Prussia from Bohemia.

Frederick had to send portions of his army to try to deal with the Russian, Swedish, and Austrian attacks. He himself, with only twenty-three thousand men, headed west in September to meet the French-German force marching through Saxony. Even though they outnumbered Frederick, they decided not to fight him, retreating westward. Frederick turned and began hurrying back to see what he could do to prevent the other invasions of Prussia.

By now it was October. Frederick received word that Austrian cavalry had entered Berlin, the Prussian capital, and had done some looting, demanded a ransom for not burning the city, and ridden off unharmed. Prussia seemed on the verge of being conquered. But Frederick was determined to save it—and Frederick had shown that he was one of the most skillful soldiers in history.

With Frederick gone from in front of them, the French-German Army began to move toward Prussia once more. Frederick quickly turned his army about and on November 4 was facing the French-German

Catherine the Great, empress of Russia, worked to increase the power and size of her nation.

troops near the town of Rossbach, in Saxony. This time, the French and German commanders, deciding that they outnumbered the Prussians almost two to one, moved forward to do battle. Their plan was to swing wide around the left flank of Frederick's position and come at him from behind. At about 11:30 in the morning on November 5, 1757, they marched forward with drums beating and bands playing.

Frederick Springs a Surprise

Frederick had men watching the enemy's every move from church towers and roofs of buildings in Rossbach. They reported that there were no scouts out either ahead of, or to the sides of, the marching army. Frederick sent most of his heavy cavalry around behind a hill called the Pölzen that the enemy troops would have to pass on their way toward Rossbach, and hid some men at the top of the hill to signal when the enemy was passing. On another nearby hill, the Janus, he placed eighteen cannons in a long line just behind the hill's crest. They could not be seen from below, but when they opened fire, their cannonballs would come down right where the enemy troops would be. He put his infantry battalions behind the guns, on the slope of the hill where they, too, were hidden from sight.

At about 3:30, the French-German Army was moving past the Pölzen, with its cavalry in front and the infantry strung out behind. At a signal from the watchers up at the top of the hill, the Prussian cavalry commander, General Frederick von Seydlitz, led his troops up the side of the hill at a quick trot. Seydlitz was smoking a pipe, and when he reached the top of the hill and saw the enemy troops below him, he pulled the pipe out of his mouth and flung it into the air, as the signal to charge. The thirty-eight squadrons of Prussian heavy cavalry, about four thousand horsemen, came thundering down the hill. They smashed into the side of the French and German cavalry, utterly shattering it and driving it in all directions. This left only the enemy infantry on the field.

The Prussians then rode off some distance behind the infantry and formed up for another charge. Moments later, the Prussian artillery opened up with a thunderous roar that actually shook the ground for a mile around. Cannonballs began tearing holes in the enemy infantry. As the French and German soldiers desperately scurried to get out of marching formation into a battle formation, the Prussian infantry battalions appeared over the crest of the Janus. They marched mechanically forward, with musket fire blazing all along the line, slamming into the French and German ranks, knocking men down by the scores. Within fifteen minutes, the French and German soldiers were falling back in panic. Then, the Prussian cavalry came charging into them from behind, swords rising and falling without mercy.

The French and their German allies had five thousand dead and wounded, five thousand soldiers taken prisoner, and their army melted away as men deserted, hoping to save themselves. Frederick's Prussians had lost only 548 men. This threat to Prussia was over.

Another Surprise

The result of the Battle of Rossbach caused a number of things to happen. Because of its losses, France had to drop out of the war against Frederick, giving him one less opponent to worry about. The government of Great Britain was so delighted by the defeat of the French that it voted to increase the amount of money and help it was giving to Frederick.

Frederick immediately headed back into Silesia, to deal with the Austrian army that was moving toward Prussia. The Austrians, sixty-five thousand men strong to Frederick's thirty-three thousand, spread out in a line of battle five miles long, with cavalry protecting both its flanks. Frederick sent some cavalry to make a pretend attack on the Austrian right, and the Austrians immediately sent reinforcements there from the left flank, weakening it. The Prussian Army then turned right and moved behind a line of hills that kept the Austrians from being able to see it. Watching the Prussians vanish from sight, the Austrian general decided they were retreating, and was more than happy to let them go rather than fight them. "The Prussians are off," he said, "Don't disturb them!"[1]

Frederick turned his army so that it was actually marching along the entire length of the Austrian line, toward its left flank. He then used a battle maneuver he had been experimenting with, one that would not have been possible had the Prussian soldiers not been so well trained to follow the shouted commands of their officers. He swung his entire army in a vast wheeling movement that had the result of lining his battalions up one after another instead of being stretched out in a line. He was then able to attack the left end of the Austrian line with his battalions coming over the hills and smashing into the surprised Austrian battalions one at a time, with a better than two-to-one advantage.

The Austrians hastily retreated, back into the nearby village of Leuthen. They gathered in the streets and clustered in buildings for protection, their officers trying desperately to get them back into formation. Prussian battalions swarmed into the village, but at first were pushed back by the heavy fire from Austrians in houses, behind fences, and in the village churchyard. Then the Prussians began to haul cannons forward to fire into the houses and churchyard at point-blank range. After half an hour of desperate fighting, the Austrians fled out of the town as the Prussians pushed forward.

The Austrians managed to get into formations some distance beyond the town. They prepared to stand off another Prussian attack. But Frederick sent a cluster of cannons up a hill looking down onto the Austrian troops, and a storm of cannonballs began crashing into them. Again the Austrians pulled back. Prussian infantry marched menacingly after them.

The Austrian commander sent seventy squadrons of cavalry to charge the Prussians, hoping to stop them and drive them back. But Frederick had prepared for this. He had forty Prussian cavalry squadrons hidden behind the hill his cannons were on. Now, the cavalry came thundering over the hill and smashed into the side of the charging Austrians, sending them reeling in all directions and stopping their charge dead. Seeing this, the Austrian infantry battalions dissolved into a panic-stricken mass, intent only on escaping. As darkness fell, the battle ended in a tremendous victory for Frederick and his Prussians. Prussian losses were about six thousand one hundred fifty; the Austrians lost some six thousand seven hundred fifty killed and wounded and twelve thousand captured. Five days later, seventeen thousand more Austrians had surrendered. This battle, the Battle of Leuthen, was one of Frederick's greatest victories and probably the greatest victory won by any army during the entire eighteenth century. The Austrian threat to Prussia was now also over.

Meanwhile, the Russian invasion had come to a complete stop. Russian troops were unable to move on roads that had been turned into rivers of mud by the beginning of winter. The Swedes in Pomerania were also bogged down.

In July 1758, Frederick marched against the Russians with thirty-six thousand men to their forty-five thousand. Near the town of Zorndorf, Frederick attacked, hitting the Russian right flank with infantry while his cavalry smashed into the center. The Russians lost 18,500 men to the Prussians' 12,797, and retreated. Now, the Russian threat was over.

The Austrians tried again, with an invasion of Saxony. Frederick hurried there with thirty-one thousand men and met the Austrian Army of eighty thousand near the town of Hochkirch. The outnumbered Prussians were finally forced to retreat, but they had battered the Austrians so badly that they could not follow and do any damage. So although the Prussian Army had been defeated, it was still intact. The year 1758 ended with Frederick still in possession of both Saxony and Silesia. Both the Russians and Swedes had withdrawn from Prussian territory.

But the war was far from over.

Chapter 5

Victories, Defeats, and "Miracles"

As 1759 began, the whole Prussian Army numbered only about one hundred twenty-seven thousand men and was split into several small armies watching the movements of the various enemy forces. In July, one of these armies was nearly wiped out by the Russian force in East Prussia. The Russians began to move toward Prussia itself. Frederick immediately took his own small army to East Prussia and attacked the Russians. Badly outnumbered, he was seriously defeated.

Frederick now thought everything was over. There was nothing to keep the Russians from conquering Prussia. But a miracle occurred. The Russian general, Count Piotr Saltykov, decided Russian troops had done enough by themselves and should have help from the Austrians. When none was offered, he sulkily

This statue was erected in Berlin, Germany, to honor the memory of Frederick the Great, thought by some to be one of the most brilliant military leaders in history.

pulled his army back and refused to budge. When Frederick learned of this, he called it "the Miracle of the House of Brandenburg [his family]."

Thus, Frederick was able to build up his army. He withdrew into Saxony, pulling his army into the hills around Dresden. In August 1760, he took his troops to the aid of one of the small armies in Silesia. But as Frederick and his thirty thousand men made camp near a town called Liegnitz, a force of ninety thousand Austrians closed around him. In the morning, they attacked.

Frederick formed his men into battle lines, and as the Austrians advanced they were hammered by those rapid, terrifying Prussian volleys. Three Austrian attacks gained nothing but piles of bloody corpses.

Then Frederick counterattacked. A regiment of infantry and two regiments of heavy cavalry smashed into the Austrians, who withdrew.

Frederick had won the Battle of Liegnitz against overwhelming odds, but he had to keep his army in Silesia, and in October a Russian and Austrian force of thirty-five thousand men invaded Prussia and captured Berlin. They committed dreadful destruction in the city, and squeezed an enormous ransom from the city officials.

There was nothing Frederick could do. An Austrian army of fifty-three thousand men had reoccupied Saxony, and Frederick had to try to drive it out. He split his army of forty-four thousand in two, planning to hit the Austrians from the rear with about thirty-two thousand men while eighteen thousand, under General Hans von Zeiten, attacked simultaneously from the south.

A Bloody Victory, Another Miracle, an End of War

But the Austrian general suspected an attack on his rear and prepared for it. When Frederick's force struck, at about two o'clock on the afternoon of November 2, it ran into the fire of nearly four hundred cannons, and the first line of attacking Prussians was massacred. A cavalry charge was wiped out. Frederick pulled his shattered remnants back, and the Austrian general sent word to Vienna of a great Austrian victory.

Frederick, too, thought victory had gone to the Austrians. But both generals were wrong. At six o'clock in the evening, in early winter darkness, General von Zeiten's force arrived and attacked. He caught the Austrians completely by surprise and unprepared. Hearing the sounds of battle, Frederick's force quickly regrouped and reattacked. Within a few hours, a shattered Austrian army was withdrawing into the night. Like the Battle of Mollwitz, this Battle of Torgau had turned from an Austrian victory into a Prussian one. But it was one of the bloodiest of Frederick's victories. The Austrians had lost twenty thousand men, but Frederick had lost fourteen thousand.

In 1761, Frederick managed to build up his army again, and held off some Russian and Austrian moves against him. But he felt it was only a matter of time before his enemies finally joined forces and formed an army so huge he could not possibly beat it. He told a friend, "Everything seems as black as if I were at the bottom of the tomb."[1]

Then, another miracle happened. In January 1762, the Russian empress Elizabeth died and the new ruler of Russia, Peter III, was a man who admired Frederick, admired Prussia, and did not like Austrians. He signed a peace treaty with Frederick. Sweden, too, dropped out of the war. Austria now faced Prussia alone. In 1763, Maria Theresa offered peace, and the Seven Years' War came to an end.

Frederick fought almost twenty-three years of constant warfare. His first war was fought to gain Silesia, and most of the rest of his fighting was done to keep Silesia and to prevent Prussia from being overwhelmed and conquered. His warfare had the result of more than doubling Prussia's size, turning it into the major nation of Germany and one of the major powers of Europe, and keeping it free. He is regarded as one of the greatest generals in history.

But Frederick was not only a great general, he was also a truly great king. He believed that a country's government should do things to help the people. He saw to it that good roads and bridges were built throughout Prussia, canals were dug to help commerce thrive, help was given to farmers who needed it, and there was real justice in the courts for even the lowliest of the peasants.

A Theft of Land, a Final War

In 1772, Frederick joined Maria Theresa of Austria and Queen Catherine II of Russia in seizing a large amount of the territory of Poland and dividing it up among themselves. Frederick took the territory of West Prussia, which lay between his province of East Prussia and the rest of Prussia. Now, Prussia was a single territory, all joined together as it never had been before. With the gain of West Prussia, Frederick had added about twenty thousand square miles of land and about six hundred thousand new people to his kingdom. Of course, what he and the others had done was simply thievery, but they could get away with it because they were powerful and Poland was weak.

However, the people of Polish West Prussia were living in dreadful poverty, and Frederick truly believed he could make things better for them, which he actually did. He gave them much more freedom than they had ever had, changed a lot of harsh laws that had been oppressing them, drained marshes to give them more land for farming, had a large canal dug that connected rivers and helped travel and commerce, and built schools.

When the American Revolutionary War against the British king began in 1775, even though Great Britain had been Frederick's ally in the Seven Years' War, he wanted America to win. He kept track of events in America. When George Washington crossed the ice-filled Delaware River and won his surprising

This political cartoon refers to the European powers' division of Poland to gain more territory for themselves.

victories at Trenton and Princeton, Frederick was delighted. He said that what Washington had done was one of the most clever military operations in history.

In 1778, at the age of sixty-six, Frederick became involved in his last war. The ruler of Bavaria, Maximilian Joseph, died, and the man who took his place, Charles Theodore, tried to make a deal with other rulers that would have let Bavaria become part of Austria. Most of the rulers of the other German

Frederick the Great admired the military skill of American General George Washington, who led his troops across the Delaware River to ambush enemy troops during the American Revolution.

countries objected to this because it would make Austria far too powerful, but none of them felt strong enough to prevent it—except Frederick. Even though he was in dreadfully poor health, suffering from painful attacks of the disease called gout, which causes inflamed swellings in the body's joints, Frederick led an army of one hundred thousand men into Bohemia. An Austrian army came marching into Bohemia and took up a position facing the Prussian Army across a river.

Nothing much happened. The Austrians had believed Frederick was too old and sick to cause them any trouble and were astounded by his action. They did not really dare fight him, and in 1779, Maria Theresa officially gave up all claim to Bavaria. Frederick had won again, without even fighting. This war became known as "the Potato War," because the soldiers spent more time hunting for food than fighting battles. However, Frederick had decisively shown that Prussia was now capable of playing a major role in anything that went on in Europe.

What Frederick Left Behind

Frederick grew more and more sickly, but he kept working for Prussia as best as he was able. He told his brother, Prince Henry, "I shall only be left in peace when my bones are covered with a little earth."[2] One of his last official acts before he died was to sign a treaty with the United States that would help both countries' commerce.

Frederick died in his palace in 1786 at the age of seventy-four. He left Prussia a much larger country than it had been when he took it over, a major power with an army of one hundred ninety thousand men, feared in war by every European nation. Virtually every European ruler knew that he or she could not make a move to gain more power, provoke a war, or even make an alliance without considering what Prussia might do about it. Frederick never dreamed of

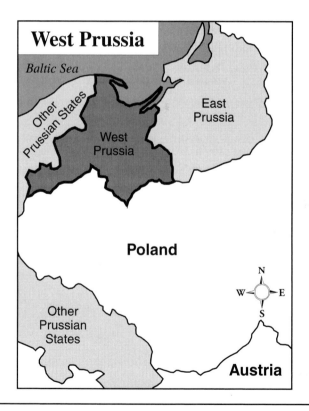

With the seizure of West Prussia from Poland in 1772, Frederick succeeded in uniting East Prussia with the other Prussian states.

trying to unify Germany, but by making a small German kingdom into one of the important countries of Europe, and turning Europe's serious attention to Germany, Frederick caused many Germans to begin thinking about the value of making all Germany as powerful and important as Prussia now was. He had laid the foundation for Germany to someday become a single, unified nation.

Napoleon Bonaparte, the self-proclaimed emperor of France, waged war to bring as much of Europe as possible under his own control.

However, things started going downhill after Frederick's death. Although other nations feared Prussia's Army, it actually began to decline. The training of the soldiers got sloppy, and discipline grew slack.

In 1799, Napoleon Bonaparte became ruler of France. Bonaparte was a military genius who began to conquer the nations of Europe. In 1806, at the Battle of Jena, Napoleon's army shattered the Prussian Army and conquered Prussia. With its main nation helpless, all Germany fell under Napoleon's control. He formed sixteen German nations, including Bavaria, Saxony, and several of Prussia's provinces, into a union called the Confederation of the Rhine. The little countries kept their rulers, but Napoleon actually ruled them all, as a single nation. It was Germany's first experience with unity.

Prussia built up its army and bided its time. Then, things started going badly for Napoleon. In 1812, he invaded Russia and was badly defeated, losing much of his army. In 1813, he was defeated again, in the Battle of Leipzig, in which the rebuilt Prussian Army took part against him.

In 1815, a baby boy was born in Brandenburg, into a land-owning Prussian noble family. He would grow up to be the man who turned Prussia into a greater power than it was in Frederick's time, and who would turn Germany into a single unified nation. His name was Otto von Bismarck.

Chapter 6

The Rise of Otto von Bismarck

On the night of July 3, 1866, eighty years after the death of Frederick the Great, a Prussian army was making camp in the Austrian town of Horitz. It was an army of conquest, for that day it had fought a battle that had actually destroyed the army of Austria, making Austria a conquered nation and turning Prussia into one of the four major powers of Europe.

Rain was pouring down on the town, and soldiers were seeking shelter where they could. A middle-aged man in the uniform of a reserve cavalry officer was not having much luck. To make matters worse, he had slipped on the muddy street and fallen into a pile of horse manure. Finally, he turned a corner and saw the town market hall, with a roofed row of columns running along the front of it, providing a narrow dry area.

Otto von Bismarck was a staunch supporter of the German monarchy. He did his best to resist popular efforts to make the country more democratic.

Hurrying into this place of shelter, he sank down with his back against a pillar and tried to go to sleep.

This drenched, shabby man, slightly stinking of horse manure, was none other than the person who had actually started the war between Prussia and Austria. He had done it with bluff and trickery, much as if he were playing a game of cards. He was Count Otto Edward Leopold von Bismarck, the prime minister of Prussia, leader of the country, appointed by the king.

When Otto von Bismarck was born on April 1, 1815, Germany was much as it had been in Frederick's time—a jumble of some thirty-eight large-to-tiny kingdoms, princedoms, and dukedoms. Napoleon Bonaparte was out of power, in exile on a tiny Mediterranean island. Eight days after Bismarck's birth, a meeting of representatives of all the Germanic countries, plus several others, officially dissolved Napoleon's Confederation of the Rhine. Instead of it, they organized all Germany, including Austria, into an alliance called the German Confederation. All the countries were still independent, but delegates from each would now meet together in a kind of congress, to try to keep things running smoothly and peaceably among them all. This was a major event. It was a step toward trying to unify Germany into a single nation with one government.

Another major event occurred several months after Bismarck's birth. Napoleon tried for a comeback. Escaping from his island prison, he took control of the French Army and made an effort to regain power. On June 18, at the Battle of Waterloo, he was defeated by two armies, one British and one Prussian, and his domination of Europe was completely ended. For its part in this victory, Prussia regained a lot of the respect and power it had lost.

Europe in 1815, the year Otto von Bismarck was born

Student, Government Worker, Soldier, Farmer

For most of his first six years, Otto von Bismarck grew up on one of his family's estates in Pomerania in northern Germany, in a countryside of open fields, woods, and streams. His father was an easygoing man, but his mother was an ambitious, rather unhappy person, who did not provide much love for Otto or his older brother, Bernhard. When he was seven, she sent him and his brother to school in the city of Berlin—which Otto hated. He preferred open country to the city.

At the age of seventeen, Bismarck entered the University of Göttingen, in the little Kingdom of Hanover, to study law. But a year later he began studies at the University of Berlin. He had a reputation as a rather wild student who often partied late into the night and fought twenty-five sword duels (carefully refereed) with other students. However, he did a great deal of reading and was quite intelligent, and in 1835, at age twenty, he passed the examination to become a lawyer.

This made Bismarck eligible to go to work for the Prussian government. He was given a civil-service job in the city of Aachen, where he worked for two years. But it was compulsory for every young Prussian man to serve in the army for a year, and Bismarck went into the service in 1838 at the age of twenty-three. During that time his mother died.

As a nobleman, Bismarck could have stayed in the army as an officer, or could have gone back to working for the government. But what he decided to do was become a farmer. In 1839, he and his brother began seeing to the cultivation of their family's vast amounts of land. For the next eight years, this was Bismarck's life.

In 1847, King Frederick William IV of Prussia decided that a railroad was needed between Berlin and the port city of Konigsberg in East Prussia. None of the railroad companies wanted to build such a railroad, which would not have been very profitable, so the government would have to do it. The king called together an assembly of leading citizens from all parts of Prussia to discuss how to raise money to pay for the railroad. One of the men selected to be a delegate to the assembly, called the United Diet (council), was Otto von Bismarck.

Things did not turn out as the king had hoped. The idea known as socialism, which taught that common people deserved more power in government, was gaining strength throughout Europe at that time, and some of the men chosen as delegates to the United Diet believed in it. They began to speak out against the king's authority, demanding a constitution for Prussia that would put more power in the hands of the people.

Revolution and Politics

Bismarck did not agree with such things. On May 17, he stood up in the assembly and made a speech—his first speech—defending the king's right to rule and denouncing anyone who spoke against it. Bismarck had shown that he was a firm monarchist who believed that only the king could decide what was best for the country.

The United Diet did not accomplish what the king wanted and he ended it after two months. Bismarck went home, and on July 28, got married to Johanna von Puttkamer, the daughter of another Prussian nobleman.

In 1848, the ideas of socialism flowing through Europe flared into actual revolutions in some places. The people of France threw out their king and made France into a republic. In Austria, the ruling emperor was forced to give up his throne, and the new emperor had to permit many changes, giving people more say in the government. There were flare-ups throughout many of the German nations, especially in Prussia. King Frederick William virtually became a prisoner in his own palace, with crowds rioting in the streets outside, demanding a constitution for Prussia.

Bismarck hurried to Berlin, convinced that only he could save the Prussian monarchy. He met with military leaders and members of the royal family, offering schemes and plans. But then, the king ordered the United Diet to reassemble for the purpose of creating a Prussian constitution and a Prussian parliament that would take over many of the powers that had belonged only to the king. Frederick William had given in to the revolution.

Bismarck was crushed, believing that the Prussian monarchy was destroyed. Inasmuch as he was still officially a member of the United Diet, he went to its first meeting on April 4, 1848. He made another speech, condemning what had taken place.

There were many other Prussian nobles and military leaders who felt just as Bismarck did, and they saw that they could count on him to help defend the Prussian monarchy. They began helping Bismarck along. When a Prussian parliament was formed, Bismarck was elected to serve in it even though he did not really support it.

In 1851, he was appointed a delegate to represent Prussia in the German Confederation Parliament, which met in the city of Frankfurt in western Germany. The main power of the confederation, which generally controlled everything that was done throughout Germany, was Austria. Austria was one of the four major nations of Europe, which also included France, Russia, and Great Britain. It was the head of an empire that consisted of today's Austria, Hungary, Slovakia, the Czech Republic, parts of what is now Yugoslavia, a section of Poland, and a section of Italy. Bismarck went to Frankfurt believing that Prussia could work with Austria for the betterment of all the German states, but he soon began to feel that Austria was interested in doing only what was best for Austria. He began working to prevent Austria from having its way in the confederation. As he told a newspaper reporter some years later, "I became its declared enemy."[1]

Prime Minister of Prussia

Bismarck continued to be given important jobs for the Prussian government. In 1859, he was made ambassador to Russia. In 1861, the Prussian king Frederick William IV died and his brother became King William I. In 1862, he appointed Bismarck ambassador to France for a short time.

But the new king had some problems and needed someone to help solve them. He wanted to increase the size of the army, but many members of the parliament were against this. By now, Bismarck was widely experienced in dealing with the governments of other nations and had become very skillful in getting the Prussian Parliament to do as he wished. There was simply no better man to take control of Prussian affairs and see that Prussia became powerful and prosperous. In 1862, King William appointed Bismarck prime minister of Prussia.

This meant that Bismarck was now the most powerful man in Prussia after the king. He was in charge of everything that Prussia did. This put him in a position

Source Document

. . . It is true that we can hardly escape complications in Germany, although we do not seek them. Germany does not look to Prussia's liberalism, but to her power. The south German States—Bavaria, Würtemberg, and Baden—would like to indulge in liberalism, and because of that no one will assign Prussia's role to them! Prussia must collect her forces and hold them in reserve for an opportune moment, which has already come and gone several times. Since the Treaty of Vienna, our frontiers have not been favorably designed for a healthy body politic. Not by speeches and majorities will the great questions of the day be decided—that was the mistake of 1848 and 1849—but by iron and blood.[2]

In 1862, Otto von Bismarck made his famous "Blood and Iron" speech.

to work for what he believed was the most important thing in the world—to make Prussia the main power of all the German states, and to unite the states into a single nation under the rule of a Prussian emperor.

He felt there was only one way to do this. In one of the first speeches he made as prime minister, Bismarck showed he believed that nations could only settle their problems with war. He declared, "The great questions of today will be settled not by speeches and majority votes . . . but by iron and blood!"[3] What he meant by "iron and blood" was, of course, warfare.

So, Bismarck set out on a path of using war to make Prussia the leader of the German nations and to make Germany a major world power. He began by causing a war in order to steal something from the Kingdom of Denmark.

Chapter 7

The War Against Denmark

The nation of Denmark is formed of several hundred various-sized islands clustered around a narrow peninsula, called Jutland, that sticks out into the sea from the coast of Germany. Although part of Denmark is attached to Germany, it was never a German nation. Its language and culture are like those of Sweden and Norway. However, there were two areas of Germany that had long been ruled by Denmark and formed the southern part of that nation. These were the duchies of Schleswig and Holstein, on the border of the German kingdom of Hanover. Most people of Holstein, and almost half the people of Schleswig, spoke German. It was an annoyance to most members of the German Confederation that the two duchies were part of Denmark, but the Danish king, Frederick VII, had clear legal right to rule them.

They had belonged to his family for centuries. However, Frederick was the last of his family. When he died in 1863, the new king, Christian IX, had no legal right to Schleswig-Holstein. He refused to give them up, however.

The German Confederation exploded with rage. Bismarck saw that the time was right to begin his plans. To Austria's astonishment, he proposed an alliance, with Prussia and Austria joining in a military operation to force Denmark to give up the duchies. Austria agreed, unaware that Bismarck wanted its assistance only to help further the needs of Prussia. But some Austrian politicians were suspicious. "Why are we acting with Prussia? Is Prussia anywhere our friend?" one demanded.[1]

The structure of an army had changed a great deal since the time of Frederick the Great. The smallest fighting force was still the battalion, of about one thousand men, with three battalions forming a regiment. But in the Prussian Army of 1864, two regiments were put together to form a brigade, two brigades formed a division, two divisions formed a corps of about twenty-four thousand infantrymen, and several corps were put together to make up an army. Thus, while Frederick had generally fought with a single army of thirty or forty thousand men, a general might now command an army of as much as one hundred thousand soldiers. A nation would put groups of such armies, totaling two hundred thousand or three hundred thousand men, into the field.

However, Prussia and Austria had no need for an army of such size, for little Denmark's army was only forty thousand men. Austria provided a single corps, and Prussia provided a corps and a division. In January 1864, this force of about fifty-six thousand men, plus a small Austrian naval force, invaded Danish territory.

Warfare in the Mid-1800s

Warfare had changed since the time of Frederick the Great. Battalions no longer marched in step toward an enemy. Now they moved quickly, often at a run. When firing at an enemy, the men often spread out a little and tried to find cover, firing from behind a tree, or kneeling behind a clump of brush. However, there was still no attempt to use camouflage or have uniforms that helped a soldier blend into the greens and browns of open country. Uniforms were still brightly colored. The Prussian infantry still had dark blue coats, with red cuffs and collars, and long gray trousers with a red stripe down the sides. Their headgear was a helmet of shiny black leather with an eagle emblem on the front, a spike on the top, and a chin-strap, all of shiny golden metal. The Austrians still wore white coats with collars and cuffs of various colors. Their trousers were sky blue, and their headgear was a tall conical cap with a visor and a golden metal emblem on the front. Danish soldiers wore a light blue uniform, but generally wore a gray overcoat over it, which helped camouflage them somewhat. Their headgear was a round flat-topped cap much like that worn by American troops in the Civil War.

The Danish Army was armed with muzzle-loading rifles. These still had to be loaded in the same way as the muskets of Frederick the Great's army, by inserting a cartridge into the muzzle and pushing it down into the firing chamber with a ramrod. However, this weapon had a range of about six hundred seventy yards, much better than in Frederick's time. The Austrian troops had a very similar kind of rifle. But the Prussians had the greater advantage of up-to-the-

The enemy knew Prussian soldiers were near when they saw the Prussians' spike-topped helmets coming toward them through the smoky battlefield.

minute technology. Since 1841, Prussia had been equipping its soldiers with a breech-loading rifle. This had a mechanism that enabled a soldier to open up the firing chamber, put a cartridge into it, and close it for firing, all in a few seconds. It had a shorter range than the muzzle loader—about six hundred yards—but it could fire five rounds during the time it took a muzzle loader to fire one.

Despite this advanced weapon, Prussian forces did not do well at first, mainly because their commander, General Field-Marshal Baron Friedrich von Wrangel, simply was not a very good general. The Chief of Staff of the Prussian Army, General Helmuth von Moltke, had produced a brilliant plan for surrounding the Danish Army and quickly ending the war in just a few days. But von Wrangel botched up the plan so badly that the Danes were able to pull back into a long line of fortifications called the Dybböl, in Schleswig, blocking the way into the rest of the peninsula. For the next two months the Danes held on in the Dybböl, preventing the Prussians and Austrians from moving forward.

General Von Moltke Takes Over

Realizing Wrangel's lack of ability, Bismarck urged the king to send General von Moltke to help him out. Moltke would eventually be recognized as one of the great military geniuses of history. He could almost instantly see all the possibilities of a situation and quickly decide the best course of action to take.

General von Moltke played a vital role in winning wars for Otto von Bismarck.

Bismarck said of him that he was "unconditionally reliable and, at the same time, cold to the very heart."[2] What he meant by this was that Moltke could be relied on for excellent judgment, and would not waiver once his mind was made up.

On April 18, Prussian artillery opened up and began smashing holes in the high wall that lay at the bottom of the fortified hills forming the Dybböl. The Prussian Royal Guard Division stormed through the wall and up into the hills, attacking the Danish positions and capturing the Dybböl. Danish forces had eighteen hundred men killed and wounded and thirty-four hundred taken prisoner; Prussian casualties were light. The stunned Danish Army fell back and withdrew onto the island of Als, off Jutland's east coast. This prevented the Prussians and Austrians from moving on into Jutland, because if they did, the Danes could come back onto Jutland *behind* them and attack from the rear. However, with the Danish Army gone, Jutland was now conquered.

Great Britain now made a diplomatic attempt to halt the fighting and settle things, with a peace conference. Bismarck sent delegates to the conference, but he worked behind the scenes to prevent any settlement. He wanted a decisive military victory that no one could dispute.

Moltke gave him the victory he needed. While the conference was going on, Moltke drew up a plan for an amphibious invasion of Als by troops in boats. When the peace conference broke up at the end of

June, Moltke launched his attack. A Prussian force in hundreds of flat-bottomed boats landed on the coast of Als, catching the Danes by surprise. The invasion was a complete success, with the Danes losing ten times more men than the invading Prussians. By July 20, Denmark was desperately seeking peace, at any cost. On September 30, with Prussian troops occupying Schleswig and Austrian troops in Holstein, Denmark was forced to sign a treaty giving up the two duchies plus the adjoining Duchy of Lauenburg. This was a loss of two fifths of its territory.

Manufacturing a War

Bismarck was intent on expanding the size of Prussia and bringing north Germany under Prussian control, with Austria pushed out of the way once and for all. The best way to do this was by defeating Austria in a war. He consulted with Moltke and other army commanders, and found they were sure that in a war, Prussia could quickly defeat Austria and any German-Confederation troops that might try to help it. But Moltke suggested that it would be helpful if Prussia had an ally. So Bismarck made a secret treaty with Italy, Austria's main enemy, which agreed to go to war with Austria if Prussia did.

Bismarck began working to make Schleswig-Holstein part of Prussia, which would add valuable land to the kingdom and hopefully anger Austria to the point of declaring war. The Austrians protested and argued, but held back from starting an actual conflict. Finally, to push Austria into war, Bismarck arranged to have a small Prussian army enter Holstein and simply force the Austrian troops there to leave.

Austria could not ignore such a challenge. On June 14, in the Confederation Parliament, Austrian delegates demanded a vote for war against Prussia. Bavaria, Saxony, Hanover, and several smaller states voted with Austria. The next day, Prussia declared war on each of these nations, and Italy declared war on Austria. Bismarck had gotten the war he wanted.

The Humbling
of Austria

Even before war was declared, Prussia and Austria began to mobilize, bringing battalions together to form regiments; forming regiments into divisions, corps, and armies; and moving the armies toward the enemy borders.

The main weapon of Austria and its German allies was still a muzzle-loading rifle. The Prussian breech-loading rifle was a much better weapon. Not only could it fire five times faster, but it could also be fired by men lying flat on the ground, which made them hard to see and shoot at. The Austrians had to stand while loading their rifles, which made them much easier targets to hit. (The Austrian Army had considered arming itself with breechloaders, but decided it would be too expensive.) Austrian artillery consisted of muzzle-loading cannons, which fired exploding projectiles for a distance of up to

2.5 miles. But about one third of the Prussian artillery was breech-loading weapons that could fire faster and farther—about 3.5 miles—than the Austrian ones.

The Prussian and Austrian armies had different ways of fighting. The Austrians believed in forming their one-thousand-man battalions into twenty ranks of fifty men each and launching them in swift-moving attacks, with bayonets thrust out, to smash into an enemy force. But the Prussian infantrymen, like the infantrymen of Frederick the Great, were trained to shoot, mowing down their enemy with steady, well-aimed rifle fire.

General von Moltke believed in keeping up with the newest technology. He had sent several Prussian Army officers to America to observe how the Union and Confederate troops fought the Civil War, and these men sent back reports of how the Union Army had made use of railroads to move troops quickly, and how American armies had used the telegraph to send orders and information to troops that were far from their headquarters. The telegraph, which was developed in England and the United States in the 1830s, was the first kind of device for sending messages a long distance by means of electricity carried across wires strung between tall poles. By pressing a switch, an operator could send electrical impulses that caused a distant switch to click at the other end. Using groups of clicks to represent letters of the alphabet, any message could be sent for miles. Accordingly, Moltke used five Prussian railroads to speedily rush troops to the borders, and used telegraphic communication to keep in touch with his forces.

Invasions

The Prussian force was divided into three armies. The First Army, of ninety-four thousand men, commanded by Prussian Prince Frederick Charles, stood on the border of the Austrian province of Bohemia. Many miles to the east, the Second Army, of one hundred twenty thousand men under Prussian Crown Prince Frederick William, was in Silesia, ready to come through the mountains into Bohemia. The forty-five-thousand-man Army of the Elbe, under General Herewarth von Bitterfeld, was at the border of Austria's ally, the Kingdom of Saxony. A fourth force of three divisions was in the western Prussian provinces, ready to deal with the other Austrian allies: Hanover, Hesse-Kassel, and Bavaria.

The day war was declared, two Prussian divisions rushed into Hanover and one went into Hesse-Kassel. One day later, the Army of the Elbe marched into Saxony. The Saxon Army of thirty-two thousand men retreated right out of its country into Bohemia. The Saxons linked up with an Austrian corps, forming a force of about fifty thousand men, which took up a defensive position on hills overlooking a town called Gitschin, about eighteen miles from the border. There they waited for the main Austrian army of about one hundred ninety thousand to join them.

On June 22, Moltke began bringing his three armies into Bohemia. He did not have any kind of plan for what he would do when his armies encountered the Austrians. He knew that such plans generally become worthless once fighting begins—there are simply too many unforeseen things that could happen. Moltke

Otto von Bismarck is still remembered as one of the strongest leaders in German history.

would just wait until his forces found the main Austrian army and then he would decide what to do.

However, the Austrian commander, the elderly Field Marshal Ludwig von Benedek, had halted his army about 28 miles from Gitschin, and he was working out a plan. He had learned the Prussian Second Army was coming down the mountains from Silesia, and decided to send several corps to meet them as they came through the narrow mountain passes. Then he would take the rest of the army to join the Austrian-Saxon force at Gitschin, which would enable him to outnumber the Prussians coming that way.

Prussian Victories

On June 27, the Austrian corps met the Second Army coming down from the mountains. Two separate battles were fought, one going to the Prussians and one to the Austrians. The Austrian losses were more than eleven thousand to the Prussians' three thousand. The Austrians fell back. On that same day, the Prussian force in Hanover attacked the Hanoverian Army. The Prussians took terrible losses but managed to surround the Hanoverians, cutting off their supplies. The next day the Prussians coming through the mountains attacked the Austrian forces trying to block them. They inflicted another ninety-five hundred casualties and sustained twenty-two thousand of their own. The Austrians pulled back again, and the Second Army kept on coming.

On June 29, the Prussian First Army attacked the Saxon-Austrian force at Gitschin. The Prussians were pushed back several times, but the Saxons and Austrians were badly outnumbered and decided to retreat. The Prussians attacked as the Saxons and Austrians were retreating, catching them massed together and unable to fight. The Austrians and Saxons finally got away but lost seven thousand men to the Prussians' two thousand. On this same day, with its supplies cut off, the Hanoverian Army was forced to surrender.

Field Marshal von Benedek was near despair. He had lost more than twenty-seven thousand men and gained nothing, and one of Austria's allies was out of the war. He sent a message to the Austrian emperor, Franz Josef, urging him to seek peace. The emperor ordered him to keep fighting.

On July 2, the Prussian king, William, came to the First Army. Bismarck was with him. Bismarck was a major in the Prussian 7th *Landwehr* (national guard) heavy cavalry regiment, and he wore his uniform at all times. It included a metal helmet with a huge spike on the top. Many of the army officers found this amusing, feeling that Bismarck was "playing soldier." One of Moltke's staff officers sarcastically referred to him as, "the civilian in the cuirassier's coat."[1] However, Bismarck felt that his life would be over if Prussia did not win this war. He had made up his mind that if it looked as though Prussia would lose, he was going to find a Prussian cavalry regiment that was about to make a charge and try to get himself killed by becoming part of it.[2]

Bismarck was concerned about the king being with the army. When he learned there might be enemy troops only six miles from where the king was going to spend the night, he asked Moltke if this was not rather dangerous. The soldier probably found this amusing.

"Yes, in war everything is dangerous," he pointed out.[3]

Bismarck liked to dress in military clothes, to show his association with Prussian troops.

An Austrian Mistake

Field Marshal von Benedek pulled all his forces together on high ground behind the Elbe River. When Moltke realized this, he instantly saw the possibility of surrounding the Austrians and squeezing them into a helpless mass. He sent orders to all his commanders. At dawn on the morning of July 3, in pouring rain, an attack was launched.

The Prussian First Army advanced toward a little town in the hills called Lipa, where two Austrian corps were in position. The Austrians had placed their artillery on hilltops overlooking fairly open ground that the Prussians would have to advance through. The Austrian officers had carefully worked out the ranges—distances—to each area of the ground. As the Prussian infantry came into range, the guns opened up with murderous fire, shells bursting all among the masses of troops. Unable to keep moving through this fire that could have wiped them out, the Prussians pulled back out of range. They huddled among the trees in a small forest, unable to move either forward or back.

Meanwhile, about five miles to the south, the front units of the Army of the Elbe were moving forward in a curve, to try to come around the left side of the Austrian positions. But the army commander, General von Bitterfeld was being very cautious, and the Prussians moved quite slowly.

King William of Prussia became concerned. "Moltke, Moltke, we are going to lose the battle!" he exclaimed.[4] Moltke was unworried. "Today Your Majesty will not only win the battle, but the entire campaign," he predicted calmly.[5]

Benedek felt that things were going well. He had plenty of troops in front of the Army of the Elbe, to hold it off on the left. He also had troops in position on the right to stop the Prussian Second Army if it showed up. With his right and left flanks safe, he planned to launch a savage counterattack in the center, against the Prussian First Army troops pinned down in front of Lipa.

Benedek's plan might have caused serious trouble for the Prussians, but two of his officers ruined it. The commanders of the troops that had been put in place to block the advance of the Prussian Second Army moved their forces out of their position into what they thought was a better one. Thus, when the Prussian Second Army finally began to arrive, there was nothing in its way. The Second Army swept forward, moving against the wide-open flank of the Austrian corps that had changed position. The Prussian breech-loading rifles began to open up, building to a steady thunder of fire pouring into the startled Austrians.

The Battle of Königgrätz

Benedek began getting reports of what was happening on his right. He suddenly realized his army was in danger of being engulfed by a double envelopment—troops moving against both his left and right flanks at the same time. His plan to launch an attack against the

Prussian troops in the center was now useless; instead of attacking, he had to move his army back, out of danger. He sent messengers out to all his commanders, ordering them to pull their troops back toward the

Emperor William I and his generals are seen here on horseback.

town of Königgrätz. He hoped to bring all his forces together there and form a new line of defense.

The Austrians began pulling back. The Prussians were moving forward everywhere. The Austrian soldiers were intent only on getting away, getting out of range of the Prussian rifles and the thundering Prussian cannons, moving as far and fast as they could before Prussian cavalry came charging into them from behind, hacking and stabbing with their swords and lances. The Austrian army became a mixed-up, fleeing mass that was no longer capable of fighting a battle. Exhausted by fighting all day, the Prussian soldiers sank to the ground wherever they were, to rest, to bind their wounds, to doze, to gobble some food if they could.

Thus, the Battle of Königgrätz came to an end. The Austrians had lost forty-five thousand men, a little more than half of them killed or wounded, the rest taken prisoner. The Prussians had lost about ten thousand.

Bismarck, at the side of King William, had spent the whole day riding from place to place to see how the battle was going. Both of them were hardly ever off their horses for thirteen straight hours. Finally, with the battle over, officers of the king's staff found the king a place to sleep in a farmhouse. It was then that Bismarck went looking for a place to sleep and wound up with his back against a column in front of the town marketplace.

The next day, an Austrian field marshal came to the headquarters of Prussian Prince Frederick Charles to ask for an armistice—an end to the fighting. Austria was surrendering. Bitterly, the field marshal told the prince that Austria no longer had an army. "It is as good as destroyed!" he declared.[6]

The Elimination of Austria

It was up to Bismarck to conduct the negotiations with the Austrian officials. But he had some serious problems to overcome first. General von Moltke wanted to pursue the remains of the Austrian Army and make sure it was completely destroyed. Also, King William wanted to take large areas of land away from Austria and add them onto Prussia. Bismarck had to argue and plead to prevent either of these things. He did not want to turn Austria into a truly bitter enemy that would be seeking revenge. He merely wanted to establish Prussia, rather than Austria, as the main power of all German-speaking countries.

He was finally able to get both Moltke and the king to agree with him. There were no further battles and Prussia did not demand any territory from Austria. Austria was simply forced to agree that it would no longer take part in any affairs of the German countries.

The 126-year rivalry that had existed between Prussia and Austria since the time of Frederick the Great had been settled, with Prussia now in control of the German states. The defeated German countries of Hanover, Nassau, and Hesse-Kassel, which had sided with Austria, were taken over as part of Prussia, and so were the two dukedoms of Schleswig and Holstein. The other states of northern Germany were formed into what was called the North German Confederation, under Prussia's leadership. Prussia was beginning to unify Germany.

Bismarck had won his gamble. Prussia, not Austria, was now one of the four major powers of Europe—and a power to be feared.

Chapter 9

The Destruction of an Empire

In the year 1870, the nation of France was the heart of a vast empire. It controlled parts of northwest and central Africa, many islands in the West Indies, a region on the coast of South America, a number of islands in the South Pacific Ocean, and much of Southeast Asia. The emperor who ruled over France and its far-flung empire was a man known as Louis Napoleon, or Napoleon III. He was the nephew of the great conqueror, Napoleon Bonaparte, who had been France's first emperor.

Bismarck discovered that as Prussia was preparing for the war against Austria, Napoleon III had made a secret agreement with the Austrian emperor that could have caused Prussia serious trouble. Bismarck decided that France could not be trusted and would have to be made powerless to ever again be a threat to Prussia.

In 1868, a revolution in Spain forced the royal family to leave the country. The Spanish government began looking among the royal houses of Europe for a new king. The position was offered to Prince Leopold Hohenzollern, the nephew of the king of Prussia. On June 19, 1870, with the approval of Bismarck and King William, Prince Leopold decided to accept.

Source Document

One brigade killed the passers-by from the Madeleine to the Opéra, another from the Opéra to the Gymnase; another from the Boulevard Bonne Nouvelle to the Porte Saint-Denis; the 75th of the Line having carried the barricade of the Porte Saint-Denis, it was no longer a fight, it was a slaughter. The massacre radiated—a word horribly true—from the boulevard into all the streets. It was a devil-fish stretching out its feelers. Flight? Why? Concealment? To what purpose? Death ran after you quicker than you could fly.[1]

Famous author Victor Hugo wrote this description of the violence with which Napoleon III's troops put down resistance to his rule in Paris in 1851.

When news of this leaked out, the French were enraged. France was sure it was another of Bismarck's plots and regarded it as a serious danger. If the king of Spain was a Prussian and France ever had to fight a war against Prussia, it might find itself attacked by Spain as well. The French ambassador in Prussia was ordered to go to King William and demand that Leopold withdraw his acceptance or France would be forced to consider the possibility of war. This was exactly what Bismarck wanted. He believed that in order for the movement toward unification of Germany to continue, it was essential to have war with France.[2] He felt this would bring Germany together as nothing else could. Most Germans hated France, whose armies had arrogantly marched through Germany a number of times during the past two hundred years. Bismarck knew that all the North German Confederation would side with Prussia, and he had made treaties with the south German nations to support each other in a war. All Germany would be united in a war against France.

However, it looked as if Bismarck's hopes would be shattered. Seeing the trouble it was causing, Prince Leopold announced he was refusing the Spanish offer.

Bismarck Manufactures Another War

But as it turned out, that was not enough for France. The French government decided it had to humiliate Prussia. The French ambassador was now ordered to demand a promise from King William that such a thing would never be allowed to happen again.

King William was taking a small vacation in the resort town of Ems. The ambassador, Count Vincente Benedetti, went there to present the demands. William assured him that France need have no worries, but Benedetti continued to demand a definite statement that would be almost an apology. Finally, apparently growing angry, the king stated that he had said everything he was going to say and did not wish to speak to Benedetti any further.

Bismarck, of course, had an agent at Ems, watching what was going on. The agent sent him a telegram, describing what had happened.

Bismarck was having supper in his home with Moltke and the Prussian minister of war, General Albrecht von Roon, when the telegram arrived. He read it, and then changed it just a bit. He made it sound as if the king had refused to speak to the French ambassador at all, and was thus refusing to even listen to the French government's demands. Bismarck felt sure that if the people of France could read his version of what had happened, it would seem to them as if France had been insulted. He took steps to have the changed telegram reproduced in newspapers throughout Europe, and had copies of it sent to all the governments of Europe. He was positive the French would be so humiliated and enraged by having all Europe learn of the insult, that they would declare war. He assured von Roon and Moltke that war was certain.

Moltke was seventy years old, but he suddenly seemed much younger and became quite excited. Slapping himself on the chest, he declared, "If I may but live to lead our armies in such a war, then the devil may come directly afterwards and fetch away the 'old carcass'. . . ."[3]

Bismarck turned out to be absolutely right. When the telegram he had altered was printed in French newspapers, crowds thronged the streets of Paris, calling for war. The French Army began to mobilize, and on July 19, 1870, France declared war. Once again, Bismarck had gotten the war he wanted.

The French Army Finds Itself Unprepared

Prussia and the states of the North German Confederation began to mobilize. The south German states of Bavaria, Württemberg, and Baden also mobilized, to join forces with the north. The army that formed to fight France was an army representing all of Germany.

Under Napoleon III, the French Army had fought in Russia, North Africa, Italy, and Mexico, and was generally regarded as being the best army in the world. Most of Europe believed the French would beat Prussia fairly easily. British newspapers predicted that the French Army would invade Germany in the region of the Rhineland and defeat the German forces in a single decisive battle.

French Emperor Louis Napoleon, or Napoleon III (pictured), ruled a vast empire. But the defeat of France by Prussia destroyed the French Empire and enabled Bismarck to create a German one.

But the fact was, the French Army was really not at all prepared for a war. The plans that had been made for bringing all the troops together with enough supplies and equipment were not well thought out. Everything began to go wrong. Many French soldiers were reservists. They were civilians most of the time and were notified to join their regiments only now that war was declared. A lot of these men were sent to the wrong places, where they simply sat and waited. As a result, many battalions and regiments were short of men. A large quantity of supplies and ammunition was also being sent to the wrong places, where no one knew what to do with them and just piled them up to gather dust. When Napoleon got to where the French divisions and corps were supposed to be coming together, he saw at once that everything was going wrong. He sent a message to the empress, telling her, "Nothing is ready. We have not troops enough."[4]

Nevertheless, the French advanced toward the German border. They did not, however, cross it, coming to a stop at the Saar River. There they stayed for the next four days, while Napoleon and his generals tried to decide what to do.

In Germany, mobilization of the armies was quick and efficient—it had been thoroughly planned by Moltke. The German railroads brought hundreds of thousands of men forward to the border. The German armies were able to form quickly, and soon began moving into France. Germany, not France, was the invader.

The Differences Between the Two Armies

The German forces marched into France in three armies. The First Army, of sixty thousand, was an all-Prussian force commanded by General Karl von Steinmetz. The Second Army, of one hundred seventy-five thousand men, commanded by Prince Frederick Karl of Prussia, was made up mainly of Prussians, but also included a corps from the Kingdom of Saxony. The Third Army, under the command of Crown Prince Frederick William of Prussia, was one hundred and forty-five thousand strong, composed of a Prussian corps, two Bavarian corps, and divisions from Württemberg, Baden, and several of the small northern German states. All three armies were under the command of Field Marshal von Moltke. Once again, both Bismarck and the king were accompanying the armies.

The Prussian soldiers looked the same as they had in the war against Austria, except that now they had their gray trousers stuffed into knee-length black boots. The soldiers from most of the other German countries looked much like the Prussians, except that instead of the black, spike-tipped helmets, some wore visored caps. But the Bavarians looked strikingly different, with light blue uniforms and black helmets with curved crests rather than spikes.

The French forces were formed into two armies, one commanded by Field Marshal Achille Bazaine, the other by Field Marshal Patrice MacMahon. The

French soldiers wore a colorful uniform of long blue coats, red trousers, white leggings, and flat-topped red-and-blue caps with visors. Napoleon III was supposedly in command of all French forces, but he was not really a very good general.

Prussia no longer had quite the technological advantages it had enjoyed against Austria. French infantrymen were equipped with a breech-loading rifle, the *chassepot*, considered to be the best weapon in Europe. It had a range twice as far as the Prussian rifle and fired twice as fast. The French also had a new

An artist depicted a meeting between Otto von Bismarck (right) and Louis Napoleon (left).

weapon, called a *mitrailleuse,* which was actually the first kind of machine gun to be used widely by any army. It could fire 150 bullets a minute, up to 1.8 miles.

However, the French had disadvantages they did not know about. French soldiers were not at all as well trained as the Prussians and could not use their rifles very well. Though it could fire over a mile, the mitrailleuse was useful only at very short range. And like the Austrians, the French had tried to save money on artillery, but the Prussian Army was now entirely equipped with breech-loading cannons that had a range nearly a mile more than any French gun. German forces also outnumbered the French considerably—three hundred eighty thousand to only two hundred thirty thousand.

Moltke Steers Toward Victory

On August 6, the German Third Army of Crown Prince Frederick William bumped into MacMahon's army near the French town of Wörth, and, as Moltke had ordered, instantly attacked. The fire of the French chassepot rifles caused heavy casualties to the advancing Prussian infantry, but Prussian artillery pounded the French troops until they had to withdraw from their position and fall back.

Even as the Third Army was attacking MacMahon, the German First and Second Armies went after Marshal Bazaine's army. After a day-long battle, the French had to retreat to keep from being surrounded.

The German forces were now between the two French armies, splitting them apart from each other, and altogether the French had lost 22,338 men to the Germans' 15,986. Concerned by these defeats, Napoleon III gave up all pretense of being in command and left things to his generals.

Moltke did not give the French any chance to reorganize. The German armies marched grimly after them, seeking battle. On August 16, Prince Frederick Karl's army caught up with Bazaine and a day-long battle was fought, with neither side gaining any advantage. Bazaine moved his army to a strong position near the city of Metz.

The next day, Moltke took command of German forces and attacked. It was another day-long battle, fiercely fought by both sides. At one point, German forces were almost ready to break. Moltke himself prevented this by bringing reinforcements just in time. The battle ended with Bazaine's troops bottled up in and around Metz, surrounded by two German armies.

Marshal MacMahon intended to slip around the side of the German Third Army, which was between him and Metz, and go to Bazaine's assistance. Incredibly, this was reported in French newspapers, and copies of the papers were brought to Moltke. Quickly, Moltke sent part of the Second Army to join the Third. Now, MacMahon was not only heavily outnumbered, about one hundred twenty thousand men to nearly two hundred fifty thousand, but also hemmed in on two sides. He found his army being

Empress Eugenie of France was the wife of Louis Napoleon.

pushed back away from Metz toward the northern French city of Sedan. He was slowly being surrounded.

On September 1, MacMahon tried to break out of the closing ring, but German artillery on all sides pounded the French infantry, and French cavalry attacks were shattered by the steady fire of the German infantry. King William, Bismarck, and Moltke watched the battle from a hilltop. As the French cavalry courageously charged the Prussian infantry again and again, only to be shot to pieces, the Prussian king murmured sadly, in French, "Ah, the brave people!"[5]

The Fall of the French Empire

Napoleon III realized that France was going to lose the war and his power would be over. He rode around the battlefield, trying his best to get himself killed. But although others were killed all around him, he was untouched.

The French Army began to come apart. Thousands of soldiers sought safety in a thick woods on a hill north of Sedan, but German artillery began dropping hundreds of shells among the trees. Thousands of other soldiers fled into Sedan. By early afternoon, most of MacMahon's army was bottled up in Sedan as Bazaine's army was bottled up in Metz.

Napoleon ordered a white flag of surrender to be raised over the town. He sent a French general to King William, with a message of surrender. That evening, a group of French generals met with Bismarck and Moltke, to discuss terms of surrender. The terms

Bismarck demanded were simple—the entire French Army was to surrender and become prisoners of war.

The French really had no choice. They surrendered, and the Battle of Sedan was over. About seventeen thousand French soldiers had been killed or wounded; one hundred four thousand became prisoners. German forces had lost about nine thousand men.

When word came that the emperor had surrendered, members of the French government seized control of things and announced that France was now a republic. The Empress Eugenie and the Crown Prince Louis fled to England. Eventually Napoleon III joined them there. He never again returned to France. The French Empire no longer existed. Bismarck and Moltke had shattered and destroyed it. The armies of Germany were now the most powerful force in Europe.

Chapter 10

The Unification of Germany

The Battle of Sedan had brought an end to the French Empire and destroyed the French Army. Everyone in Germany knew that the war was all but over. They were jubilant that Germany was being regarded around the world as a new major power. Most people were now talking about the need for unification. The very next day after the Battle of Sedan, Bismarck ordered his staff to begin writing a constitution for a unified German Empire, with Prussian King William as the first emperor. Meanwhile, Bismarck and his representatives had to meet with the rulers of all the little German countries, to assure them they would not be losing out if Germany was unified.

One big problem was the large Kingdom of Bavaria. For more than one hundred years, Bavaria and Prussia had been rivals. They had even fought

Unification of Germany

By 1871, Otto von Bismarck had succeeded in unifying the German states (shaded) into a single vast empire.

wars against each other several times. Even though they had fought together against France, their relationship was not good.

The Bavarian king, Ludwig II, was a rather dreamy and slightly deranged young man whose main interests were music and building fantastic castles. However, he seemed determined to see that Bavaria would not lose its importance by becoming part of an empire. Bismarck had to gently talk him out of some of his wildest ideas—such as that a Prussian and a Bavarian should alternate as emperor—and agreed to many small demands. Thus, Bavaria got to have its own separate stamps, its own coins (with Ludwig's portrait on them), and its own special uniforms for its part of the Empire's Army. Finally, Bismarck was able to walk into the room where his staff was working, and announce, "Gentlemen, the Bavarian treaty has been signed. German unity is a *fait accompli* [an accomplished fact], and our king has become the German Emperor!"[1]

However, the biggest problem still remained. William, the Prussian king, did not want to be the emperor of Germany. Bismarck had to actually bribe King Ludwig, with a large sum of money, to write a letter to William urging him to accept the position. Reluctantly, William agreed.

A United Germany, an End to the War

The French had tried to keep fighting after the Battle of Sedan, but half their force had surrendered and the other half was surrounded within Metz. However, a wave of patriotism swept the country. The new government was able to recruit more soldiers and form new armies. The Germans kept two armies in a ring around Metz. The other army marched to Paris, arriving in mid-September. Paris was heavily fortified, and Moltke did not want to waste men trying to fight his way into the city. So, he surrounded it, cutting off all delivery of supplies, and began to wait for starvation to force the city to surrender.

In October, the French Army in Metz surrendered. This freed the German troops at Metz to begin moving against the French forces that were gathering to try to gain enough strength for an attack on the Germans surrounding Paris. The French were defeated in several battles.

On January 5, 1871, the German troops outside Paris began bombarding the city with the fire of large

Source Document

In the fields on each side of the road there were numerous regiments of Mobiles drawn up ready to advance if required. The sailors, who are quartered here in great numbers, said that they had carried Le Bourget early in the morning, but that they had been obliged to fall back, with the loss of about a third of their number. . . . Little seemed to be known of what was passing. "The Prussians will be here in an hour," shouted one man; "The Prussians are being exterminated," shouted another. . . . The people on the Boulevards seem to imagine that a great victory has been gained. When one asks them where? they answer "everywhere".[2]

Henry Labouchere wrote this account of the siege of Paris by Prussian troops in 1870.

cannons, in hope of bringing about a surrender more quickly. The town of Versailles is twelve miles from Paris, where stands one of the most beautiful palaces in Europe. Within this palace is a huge room. It is known as the Hall of Mirrors because the two long walls across from each other are covered from end to end with tall, broad mirrors in ornate panels. On January 18, 1871, as the guns outside Paris were thudding away, the Hall of Mirrors was filled with the generals and commanders of the German armies, and officials of the German nations. On a platform at the center of the hall stood King William I of Prussia, with Bismarck beside him, in the uniform of a colonel of a Guard regiment. The king made a speech, accepting the position of emperor of all Germany. Bismarck read a proclamation, announcing that all the German nations were now united as a new German Empire. The room thundered with shouts and cheers. Bismarck had made his dream come true.

By February, the war was over. France was unable to fight any longer. Bismarck and Moltke met with members of the French government and worked out peace terms. The French province of Alsace (which had once been part of Germany) and part of the province of Lorraine were taken from France and became part of the German Empire. France was forced to pay an enormous amount of money, equal to about $1 billion today, to Germany.

Bismarck's Effect on History

In Europe, the outcome of the war was regarded with mixed feelings. Some Europeans had become sympathetic to the French, because it appeared as if Germany had been too harsh in its surrender demands. In America, the result of the war was looked on with approval. Napoleon III had been regarded as a troublemaker—the United States had nearly had a war with France when Napoleon III tried to turn Mexico into a French-dominated empire. But Germans were regarded as hard-working, law-abiding people. Americans believed that the German victory, and a unified Germany, would help Europe stay peaceful.

From Bismarck's Triumph to the Germany of Today

Just as Frederick the Great had made Prussia into one of the foremost nations of Europe, Otto von Bismarck had created a new nation that was one of the foremost powers of the world. In just about eight years, Bismarck had turned a cluster of quarreling kingdoms, princedoms, and dukedoms into a single nation of such great military power that it was feared throughout Europe and the world.

Bismarck continued to be prime minister of all Germany for another nineteen years. But in 1888, a new young Prussian emperor, William II, took over the throne and in 1890 he requested that Bismarck resign.

Bismarck died in 1898. He had gained his goal of unification by starting three wars that had caused the deaths of many thousands of men and the crippling of

Source Document

Those who do not want to cooperate in the defense of the state do not belong to the state. They have no rights in the state. They should withdraw from the state. We are no longer so barbaric as to drive them out, but this would be the answer to give against all those who negate the state and its institutions. All the protection accorded them by the state which they negate should be withdrawn from them. In the old German Empire this was called "the ban." It is a hard judgment for which we have become too soft today. But there are no grounds to give rights in the state to those who recognize no obligations to it. . . .[1]

Bismarck laid out the principles of the government's hostile policies toward Polish people living in Germany in this 1886 speech.

many others. Bismarck always insisted that he did not feel that war was in any way glorious, and that he sincerely regretted the death and injury of soldiers.[2]

Nevertheless, such feelings had not stopped him. He had made Germany a unified country by means of warfare. For the next sixteen years after his death, the image of Germany that he had created, as an unbeatable military power, kept most of Europe uneasy. France hated Germany because of the loss of Alsace and Lorraine, and Russia feared Germany as a possible enemy. Eventually, France and Russia made an agreement to help each other if one of them was ever drawn into a war. This meant that Germany faced the possibility of someday having to fight a two-front war, against Russia in the east and France in the west.

Bismarck in his later years

Seeking to have help in such a war, Germany formed an alliance with Bismarck's old enemy, Austria.

The End of the Empire, a Changed Nation

In 1914, all these alliances forced Europe into World War I. Austria, now part of Austria-Hungary became involved in a war with Serbia. Because of an agreement with Serbia, Russia began to mobilize its army for war with Austria-Hungary. Because of its alliance with Austria-Hungary, Germany began to mobilize against Russia. And because of its alliance with Russia, France mobilized against Germany. Eventually, sixteen other nations joined Russia, Serbia, and France, including Italy, Britain, and the United States. Bulgaria and the Ottoman Empire soon allied with Germany and Austria-Hungary.

The war came to an end in 1918, with the defeat of Germany. The German emperor was forced to leave the country, taking refuge in the Netherlands. The empire that Bismarck had created was destroyed. Germany remained a single nation, but it became a republic.

In 1933, the republic was taken over by the political party known as Nazis. The Nazi leader, Adolf Hitler, became dictator of Germany and in 1939 led Germany into World War II. By 1945, Germany had been defeated again and was occupied by American, British, and French troops in the west, and by troops of the Soviet Union (communist Russia) in the east. In

1949, it split into two nations: the Federal Republic of Germany in the west, and the German Democratic Republic in the east. As a result, Prussia, the country of Frederick the Great and Bismarck, disappeared completely. Its name no longer even exists.

Germany remained two separate nations for half a century, until it was reunited in 1990. Today, it is a single nation once more, a democracy, and an important and respected member of the nations of Europe. Its image as a fearsome military power, which Frederick the Great and Otto von Bismarck fastened on it, is no longer part of its image in the world of today.

1712—*January 28:* Frederick the Great is born in Berlin.

1713—*February 25:* Frederick's father becomes King Frederick William I of Prussia.

1733—*June 12:* Frederick marries Elizabeth Christina of Brunswick-Bevern.

1740—*May 31:* Frederick William I dies; Frederick becomes King Frederick II of Prussia.

December 16: Frederick invades Silesia; First Silesian War begins.

1741—*April 10:* Frederick's army defeats an Austrian army at the Battle of Mollwitz, without Frederick present.

1742—*May 17:* Frederick wins his own first victory at the Battle of Chotusitz, defeating the Austrians.

June 11: Maria Theresa makes peace with Frederick, giving up Silesia to Prussia. The First Silesian War ends.

1744—*July 15:* Frederick invades Bohemia, beginning the Second Silesian War.

1745—*June 4:* Frederick defeats Austrian-Saxon forces at the Battle of Hohenfriedburg.

September 30: Frederick defeats Austrian forces at the Battle of Soor.

December 15: The prince of Anhalt-Dessau, a Prussian general, defeats the Austrians at the Battle of Kesselsdorf.

December 25: Maria Theresa again makes peace. The Second Silesian War ends.

1756—*August 29:* Frederick invades Saxony. The Seven Years' War begins.

October 1: Frederick defeats an Austrian army at the Battle of Lobositz.

1757—*May 6:* Frederick defeats an Austrian army at Prague and besieges the city.

June 18: Frederick is defeated at the Battle of Kolin and gives up the siege of Prague, withdrawing from Bohemia.

November 5: Frederick routes a French and German army at the Battle of Rossbach.

December 5: Frederick destroys an Austrian army at the Battle of Leuthen.

1758—*August 25:* Frederick defeats a Russian army at the Battle of Zorndorf.

October 14: Frederick is defeated by an Austrian force at the Battle of Hochkirch.

1759—*August 12:* Frederick is badly defeated by a Russian-Austrian army at the Battle of Kunnersdorf.

1760—*August 15:* Frederick defeats Austrian forces at the Battle of Liegnitz.

November 3: Frederick defeats an Austrian army at the Battle of Torgau.

1762—*January 5:* The death of the Russian empress removes Russia from the war, saving Prussia from defeat.

1763—*February 15:* All the warring nations sign a peace agreement and the Seven Years' War ends; Prussia keeps Silesia.

1772—Frederick joins with the rulers of Russia and Austria to seize territory from Poland; Prussia takes over the Polish province of West Prussia.

1778—*July 5:* Frederick leads an army into Bohemia, embarking on his last war.

1786—*August 17:* Frederick dies at the age of seventy-four.

1815—*April 1:* Otto von Bismarck is born.

June 8: The German Confederation is formed.

June 18: A Prussian army helps defeat Napoleon Bonaparte at the Battle of Waterloo.

1835—*June 4:* Bismarck takes a minor job in the Prussian government.

1847—*April 11:* Bismarck becomes a member of the Prussian king's council.

July 28: Bismarck marries Johanna von Puttkamer.

1851—*May 11:* Bismarck becomes a delegate to the German Confederation Parliament in Frankfurt.

1862—*September 23:* Bismarck is made acting prime minister of Prussia.

September 30: He makes his famous "Blood and Iron" speech.

1864—*January 18:* Prussia and Austria go to war with Denmark.

1866—*June 16:* Prussia goes to war with Austria.

July 3: Austria is defeated at the Battle of Königgrätz.

1867—*April 16:* The North German Confederation is proclaimed; Bismarck is appointed North German chancellor.

1870—*July 19:* Prussia and the other German states go to war with France.

September 4: The French Empire falls and a republic is created.

1871—*January 18:* William I is proclaimed emperor of all Germany, making Germany a single unified nation; Bismarck becomes chancellor of Germany.

1898—*July 30:* Bismarck dies at age eighty-three.

Chapter 1. The Crown Prince of Prussia

1. Ralph Flenly, *Modern German History,* 4th ed. (New York: E. P. Dutton & Co., Inc., 1968), p. 56.

2. Louis Snyder, ed., *Frederick the Great* (Englewood Cliffs, N.J.: Prentice Hall, Inc., 1971), p. 77.

3. Ibid.

4. Jackson J. Spielvogel, *Western Civilization,* 4th ed. (Belmont, Calif.: Wadsworth/Thomson Learning, 1999), p. 523.

5. Paul Halsall, "Modern History Sourcebook: Voltaire: *Patrie* in *The Philosophical Dictionary, 1752,*" *Modern History Sourcebook,* July 1998, <http://www.fordham.edu/halsall/mod/1752voltaire.html> (May 4, 2001).

6. Nancy Mitford, *Frederick the Great* (New York: Harper & Row, Publishers, 1970), p. 87.

Chapter 2. A Surprise Victory

1. David K. Koeller, "Frederick II (the Great) of Prussia Political Testament," *North Park University History Department,* 1998, <http://www.admin.northpark.edu/dkoeller/Classes/Sources/Frederick%20the%20Great.html> (November 9, 2001).

2. Nancy Mitford, *Frederick the Great* (New York: Harper & Row, Publishers, 1970), p. 100.

Chapter 3. Another War, More Victories

1. Christopher Duffy, *The Military Life of Frederick the Great* (New York: Atheneum, 1986), p. 62.

2. Louis Snyder, ed., *Frederick the Great* (Englewood Cliffs, N.J.: Prentice Hall, Inc., 1971), p. 96.

3. Duffy, p. 218.

4. Duffy, p. 72.

Chapter 4. Prussia Against Europe

1. Major General J.F.C. Fuller, *A Military History of the Western World* (New York: Funk & Wagnalls Company, 1955), Vol. 2, p. 210.

Chapter 5. Victories, Defeats, and "Miracles"

1. Nancy Mitford, *Frederick the Great* (New York: Harper & Row, Publishers, 1970), p. 238.

2. Ibid., p. 287.

Chapter 6. The Rise of Otto von Bismarck

1. Frederick B. M. Hollyday, ed., *Bismarck* (Englewood Cliffs, N.J.: Prentice Hall, Inc., 1970), p. 29.

2. Milton Viorst, ed., *The Great Documents of Western Civilization* (New York: Barnes & Noble Books, 1965), p. 265.

3. Edward Crankshaw, *Bismarck* (New York: The Viking Press, 1981), p. 133.

Chapter 7. The War Against Denmark

1. Edward Crankshaw, *Bismarck* (New York: The Viking Press, 1981), p. 171.

2. Gordon A. Craig, *The Battle of Königgrätz: Prussia's Victory Over Austria, 1866* (Philadelphia and New York: J. B. Lippincott Company, 1964), p. 24.

Chapter 8. The Humbling of Austria

1. Edward Crankshaw, *Bismarck* (New York: The Viking Press, 1981), p. 280.

2. Ibid., p. 210.

3. Gordon A. Craig, *The Battle of Königgrätz: Prussia's Victory Over Austria, 1866* (Philadelphia and New York: J. B. Lippincott Company, 1964), p. 82.

4. Günter Roth, "Field Marshal von Moltke the Elder: His Importance Then and Now," *Tactical Notebook* (Institute for Tactical Education, 1994), p. 7.

5. Ibid.

6. Craig, p. 166.

Chapter 9. The Destruction of an Empire

1. Victor Hugo, "Louis Napoleon's Troops Subdue Paris, 4 December 1851," *Eyewitness to History,* ed. John Carey (New York: Avon Books, 1987), p. 330.

2. Frederick B. M. Hollyday, ed., *Bismarck* (Englewood Cliffs, N.J.: Prentice Hall, Inc., 1970), p. 32.

3. Ibid., p. 33.

4. David Duff, *Eugenie and Napoleon III* (New York: William Morrow and Company, Inc., 1978), p. 200.

5. Michael Howard, *The Franco-Prussian War* (New York: The Macmillan Company, 1962), p. 216.

Chapter 10. The Unification of Germany

1. Alan Palmer, ed., *Nations and Empires* (New York: Newsweek Books, 1974), p. 83.

2. Henry Labouchere, "The Siege of Paris, December 1870," *The Mammoth Book of Eyewitness History,* ed. Jon E. Lewis (New York: Carroll & Graf Publishers, 1998), pp. 267–268.

Chapter 11. From Bismarck's Triumph to the Germany of Today

1. "Bismarck and the 'Polish Question': Speech to the Lower house of the Prussian Parliament, January 28, 1886," n.d., <http://www2.h_net.msu.edu/~german/gtext/kaiserreich/speech.html> (April 10, 2001).

2. Edward Crankshaw, *Bismarck* (New York: The Viking Press, 1981), p. 215.

Further Reading

Books

Booth, Martin. *Bismarck.* New York: Greenhaven, 1980.

Bradley, John, and Catherine Bradley. *Germany: The Reunification of a Nation.* Danbury, Conn.: Franklin Watts, 1991.

Dolan, Sean. *Germany.* Broomall, Penn.: Chelsea House, 1999.

Kittredge, Mary. *Frederick the Great.* Broomall, Penn.: Chelsea House, 1987.

Rose, Jonathan. *Otto von Bismarck.* Broomall, Penn.: Chelsea House, 1987.

Spencer, William. *Germany Then and Now.* Danbury, Conn.: Franklin Watts, 1994.

Internet Addresses

Allen, Ed. "Maps of Frederick the Great's Campaigns and Battles." *Frederick the Great's Campaigns and Battles.* n.d. <http://tetrad.stanford.edu/hm/FredMaps.html>.

"Otto von Bismarck—'Founder' of the German Empire." *German News.* June/July 1998. <http://www.germanembassy-india.org/news/98july/gn07.htm>.

Rempel, Professor Gerhard. "The Heritage of Bismarck." *Western New England College.* n.d. <http://mars.acnet.wnec.edu/~grempel/courses/germany/lectures/12bismarck.html>.

Index